WALKING IN NEWNESS OF LIFE

A Practical Study of
Your New Life in Jesus Christ

Study Guide
Teacher's Edition

Pastor Jeremy Markle

WALKING IN THE WORD
MINISTRIES

Pastor Jeremy Markle
www.walkinginthewordministries.net

WALK IN NEWNESS OF LIFE

A Practical Study of Your New Life in Jesus Christ

Study Guide
Teacher's Edition

All rights reserved solely by the author.
No part of this book may be reproduced, stored in a retrieval system,
or transmitted in any form or by any means –
electronic, mechanical, photocopy, recording, or otherwise –
without written permission of the author.

Unless otherwise noted, all Scripture quotations are from the King James Version.

Copyright © 2017 by Pastor Jeremy Markle

Published by Walking in the WORD Ministries
www.walkinginthewordministries.net

Printed in the United States of America

ISBN: 978-1947430013

Content

Your New Heavenly Father . . . . Study Guide - Page 1

Your New Belonging . . . . Study Guide - Page 13

Your New Comforter . . . . Study Guide - Page 27

Your New Freedom from Sin . . . . Study Guide - Page 41

Your New Spiritual Blessing . . . . Study Guide - Page 59

Your New Hope . . . . Study Guide - Page 71

Your New Focus . . . . Study Guide - Page 85

Your New Mind . . . . Study Guide - Page 101

Your New Spiritual Hunger . . . . Study Guide - Page 121

Your New Access to the Throne of Grace . . . . Study Guide - Page 137

Your Body's New Owner . . . . Study Guide - Page 151

Your New Lifestyle . . . . Study Guide - Page 163

Your New Privilege . . . . Study Guide - Page 179

Romans 6:1-13

1 What shall we say then?
Shall we continue in sin, that grace may abound?
2 God forbid.
How shall we, that are dead to sin,
live any longer therein?
3 Know ye not,
that so many of us as were baptized into Jesus Christ
were baptized into his death?
4 Therefore we are buried with him
by baptism into death:
that like as Christ was raised up from the dead
by the glory of the Father,
EVEN SO WE ALSO
SHOULD WALK IN NEWNESS OF LIFE.
5 For if we have been planted together
in the likeness of his death,
we shall be also in the likeness of his resurrection:
6 Knowing this, that our old man is crucified with him,
that the body of sin might be destroyed,
that henceforth we should not serve sin.
7 For he that is dead is freed from sin.
8 Now if we be dead with Christ,
we believe that we shall also live with him:
9 Knowing that Christ being raised from the dead
dieth no more;
death hath no more dominion over him.
10 For in that he died, he died unto sin once:
but in that he liveth, he liveth unto God.
11 Likewise reckon ye also yourselves
to be dead indeed unto sin,
but alive unto God through Jesus Christ our Lord.
12 Let not sin therefore reign in your mortal body,
that ye should obey it in the lusts thereof.
13 Neither yield ye your members
as instruments of unrighteousness unto sin:
but yield yourselves unto God,
as those that are alive from the dead,
and your members as instruments of righteousness unto God.

Prologue

An Introduction to Your New Life

Jesus Christ, while answering Nicodemus's spiritual questions, explained that only those who have been *"born again"* will be permitted to enter God's kingdom (John 3:1-21). Nicodemus then responded in confusion by asking, *"How can a man be born when he is old? Can he enter the second time into his mother's womb and be born? Jesus answered, Verily, verily, I say unto thee, Except a man be born of water and of the Spirit, he cannot enter into the kingdom of God. That which is born of the flesh is flesh; and that which is born of the Spirit is spirit. Marvel not that I said unto thee, Ye must be born again"* (John 3:4-7). Jesus Christ was teaching Nicodemus that each individual who enters heaven must have two birthdays: a physical and a spiritual one. They must first be born into a physical family, and then they must personally choose to be born into God's spiritual family by believing in Jesus Christ's death, burial, and resurrection as the only payment for their sins (John 1:12-13, Ephesians 2:1-10). Although physical life on this earth is temporal, Jesus promised Nicodemus that the spiritual life that God gives is eternal. In John 3:16-18, Jesus says, *"For God so loved the world, that he gave his only begotten Son, that whosoever believeth in him should not perish, but have everlasting life. For God sent not his Son into the world to condemn the world; but that the world through him might be saved. He that believeth on him is not condemned: but he that believeth not is condemned already, because he hath not believed in the name of the only begotten Son of God."*

Jesus Christ was sent into the world by God the Father *"to seek and to save that which was lost"* (Luke 19:10). He was sent to give spiritual life to those who were *"dead in their trespasses and sins"* (Ephesians 2:1). Through His finished work on the cross, He has given, *"as many as received him, ... [the] power to become the sons of God, even to them that believe on his name*" (John 1:12). Jesus Christ came to sacrifice himself so that you and I "*might have life, and that they [we] might have it more abundantly*" (John 10:10). And God has promised that "*if any man be in Christ, he is a new creature: old things are passed away; behold, all things are become new*" (II Corinthians 5:17).

Jesus Christ has not only provided the opportunity for each believer to have a new life as one of God's children, but He has also left "*us an example, that ye [we] should follow his steps: who did no sin, neither was guile found in his mouth: who, when he was reviled, reviled not again; when he suffered, he threatened not; but committed himself to him that judgeth righteously*" (I Peter 2:21-23). I John 2:6 teaches that "*He that saith he abideth in him ought himself also so to walk, even as he walked.*" If a believer is truly depending on Jesus Christ for his new life, he should desire to live according to the example Jesus Christ provided him. He should say with the Apostle Paul, "*Christ liveth in me: and the life which I now live in the flesh I live by the faith of the Son of God, who loved me, and gave himself for me*" (Galatians 2:20).

The purpose of this Biblical study is to search the Scriptures to find the true significance of the "New Life" found in Jesus Christ, and to discover both the great promises and responsibilities of each of God's children as they "*walk in newness of life*" (Romans 6:4).

Chapter I

Your New Heavenly Father

John 1:12-13
But as many as received him,
to them gave he power to become the sons of God,
even to them that believe on his name:
Which were born, not of blood,
nor of the will of the flesh,
nor of the will of man,
but of God.

Chapter 1

Your New Heavenly Father

A Biblical Introduction to Your New Heavenly Father

John 1:12-13 promises that when you believe in Jesus Christ as your personal Savior, you are immediately given the power, or permission, to become a child of God the Father as it says, "*But as many as received him, to them gave he power to become the sons of God, even to them that believe on his name: Which were born, not of blood, nor of the will of the flesh, nor of the will of man, but of God.*" Galatians 3:26 confirms this promise. "*For ye are all the children of God by faith in Christ Jesus.*"

The privilege of being one of God's children involves much more than the traditions and rituals that religion can offer. It is a personal relationship with God the Father; whereby you can call Him "*Abba*" or daddy (Romans 8:15-17, Galatians 4:6). As your heavenly Father, God desires that you depend on Him for every area of your life and communicate with Him through prayer so that He can perfectly and lovingly supply for your every need through His provision, instruction, comfort, correction, etc (Matthew 6:7-14, 25-34, Luke 11:1-13).

As your Heavenly Father, God desires that you would represent Him to the world by living a righteous life. "*In this the children of God are manifest, and the children of the devil: whosoever doeth not righteousness is not of God*" (I John 3:9-10). God always has your best interest in mind, and He knows that the only way you will be able to truly enjoy your new life is when you live as an "*obedient [child], not fashioning [yourself] according to the former lusts in your ignorance: But as he which hath called you is holy, so be ye holy in all manner of conversation; Because it is written, Be ye holy; for I am holy*" (I Peter 1:14-16).

God the Father loves you so much that He is willing to fulfill his Fatherly responsibility to correct you when you are disobedient to Him (Hebrews 12:5-13). "*For whom the Lord loveth he chasteneth, and scourgeth every son whom he receiveth. If ye endure chastening, God dealeth with you as with sons; for what son is he whom the father chasteneth not*" (Hebrews 12:6-7). God the Father knows that "*Now no chastening for the present seemeth to be joyous, but grievous: nevertheless afterward it yieldeth the peaceable fruit of righteousness unto them which are exercised thereby,*" and He does not desire for you to stay discouraged following correction but rather says, "*Wherefore lift up the hands which hang down, and the feeble knees; and make straight paths for your feet, lest that which is lame be turned out of the way; but let it rather be healed*" (Hebrews 12:11-13). Your heavenly Father promises that "*if [you] confess our sins, he is faithful and just to forgive [you your] sins, and to cleanse [you] from all unrighteousness*" (I John 1:9).

I John 3:1-2 says, "*Behold, what manner of love the Father hath bestowed upon us, that we should be called the sons of God: ... Beloved, now are we the sons of God, and it doth not yet appear what we shall be: but we know that, when he shall appear, we shall be like him; for we shall see him as he is.*" Do you accept the wonderful truth that God's love for you has provided you with not only the forgiveness of your sins, but also a special place in His family as one of His children? Will you allow this truth to motivate you to honor Him every day of your life? And will you make a commitment to live your new life as one of His obedient children until the end of your life on this earth?

Biblical Instruction about Your New Heavenly Father

- ✓ **Matthew 5:14-16** - God the Father should receive glory from those who observe your life.

- ✓ **Matthew 6:1-4** - God the Father rewards His obedient children.

- ✓ **Matthew 6:6-13** - God the Father wants His children to pray to Him for their daily needs, spiritual protection, and forgiveness.

- ✓ **Matthew 6:14-15, I John 1:5-10** - God the Father forgives His children's sins.

- ✓ **Matthew 14:16-17, 26, Luke 11:13, John 14:16-18, 16, 15:26, 16:13-14, I Corinthians 2:9-16** - God the Father gives each of His children the Holy Spirit to comfort and guide them throughout their new life.

- ✓ **Romans 1:7, I Corinthians 1:3-5, II Corinthians 1:2-4, Galatians 1:3, Ephesians 1:2, Philippians 1:2, Colossians 1:2, I Thessalonians 1:1, II Thessalonians 1:2, I Timothy 1:2, II Timothy 1:2, Titus 1:4, Philemon 1:3** - God the Father gives grace, peace, and mercy to His children.

- ✓ **II Corinthians 6:16-18** - God the Father requires that His children separate themselves from the world so that He can have fellowship with them.

- ✓ **Ephesians 1:3-6** - God the Father blesses His children with spiritual blessings in heaven.

Walk in Newness of Life

- ✓ **Philippians 4:20** - God the Father deserves His children's glory for all eternity.

- ✓ **I Thessalonians 1:2-3** - God the Father observes each of His children's work of faith, labor of love, and patience of hope.

- ✓ **II Thessalonians 2:6-7** - God the Father loves His children and gives them everlasting consolation and good hope through His grace.

- ✓ _____ - _____

- ✓ _____ - _____

- ✓ _____ - _____

- ✓ _____ - _____

- ✓ _____ - _____

- ✓ _____ - _____

- ✓ _____ - _____

- ✓ _____ - _____

- ✓ _____ - _____

Biblical Investigation about Your New Heavenly Father

John 1:12-13

1. Who must you receive to become a child of God? *(John 1:1-16, 29-37)*
   <u>Jesus Christ</u>

2. Who gives you the power to be one of God's children?
   <u>Jesus Christ</u>

3. By Whose will have you become one of God's children? *(John 3:16-18, 20:31, Acts 4:12, Philippians 2:5-11)*
   <u>God's</u>

Galatians 3:26

4. In whom must you have faith to be a child of God?
   <u>Christ Jesus</u>

Romans 8:14-17
Galatians 4:4-7

5. Who leads the children of God?
   <u>The Spirit of God</u>

6. The Spirit of God is a "Spirit of <u>Adoption</u>."

7. God's children can call Him by what name?
   <u>Abba - Daddy</u>

8. If you are a child of God, you are also one of His <u>heirs</u>.

Matthew 6:7-15, 25-34
Luke 11:1-13

9. Does God want you to pray to Him about your daily spiritual and physical needs?
   <u>Yes</u>

10. If you seek first "**<u>kingdom of God, and his righteousness</u>;** ... *all these things shall be added unto you.*"

I John 3:9-10

11. What should you do to show that you are a child of God?
    ♦ <u>Do righteousness</u>
    ♦ <u>Love my brother</u>

I Peter 1:14-16

12. What type of child should you be?
    <u>Obedient</u>

13. If you are going to be like your heavenly Father, how must you live?
    <u>Holy</u>

Hebrews 12:5-13

14. What does God do to you when you disobey Him?
    - ♦ Chasten
    - ♦ Rebuke

15. What does God's chastening and scourging prove about your relationship with God?
    I am His child

16. What does God's chastening produce in your life?
    - ♦ I am a partaker of His holiness
    - ♦ The peaceable fruit of righteousness

17. What must you do after you are chastened by God?
    - ♦ Lift up my hands which hang down
    - ♦ Lift up my feeble knees
    - ♦ Make straight paths for my feet

I John 1:9

18. What has God promised He will do for you if you confess and forsake your sins?
    He will forgive me and cleanse me

I John 3:1-3

19. What does being accepted as one of God's children display about His interest in you?
    His loves me

20. What will happen to you when God returns and you see Him in His glory?
    <u>I will be like Him</u>

21. What should you do because you are one of God's children and are looking forward to seeing Him?
    <u>Purify myself</u>

Personal Notes about Your New Heavenly Father

Walk in Newness of Life

Chapter 2

Your New Belonging

Ephesians 3:6
That the Gentiles should be fellowheirs,
and of the same body,
and partakers of his promise in Christ by the gospel:

Chapter 2

Your New Belonging

A Biblical Introduction about Your New Belonging

Ephesians 3:6 explains three ways in which you have spiritual belonging as one of God's children. It says that all believers are ***"fellowheirs, and of the same body, and partakers of his promise in Christ by the gospel."***

At the moment of your faith in Jesus Christ as your personal Savior, God the Father became your Heavenly Father. He has made you a member of His family in which you are one of His heirs. Romans 8:15-17 further explains your position in God's family by saying, ***"For ye have not received the spirit of bondage again to fear; but ye have received the Spirit of adoption, whereby we cry, Abba, Father. The Spirit itself beareth witness with our spirit, that we are the children of God: And if children, then heirs; heirs of God, and joint-heirs with Christ; if so be that we suffer with him, that we may be also glorified together."*** You now belong. You belong to very special family and ***"are no more [a stranger] and [a foreigner], but [a fellow citizen] with the saints, and of the household of God"*** (Ephesians 2:19). You have a spiritual home and a spiritual family to call your own. You are even privileged to be known by a family name. God the Father is your Father, and you are known by His name because He is from ***"whom the whole family in heaven and earth is named"*** (Ephesians 3:14-15).

Another great privilege of being in a family is that you are not alone. You are a ***"fellowheirs,"*** which means you have brothers and sisters, who are also heirs and part of your family, who can help you in your times of need and rejoice with you in your times of blessing (Romans 12:15, Galatians 6:10). Because of this special relationship with God's other children, believers will often cordially refer to each other as "brother" or "sister" in the local church. The local church is a gathering of God's family, and each service is a family reunion, where brothers and sisters "*consider one another to provoke unto love and to good works*" (Hebrews 10:24-25).

Second, Ephesians 3:6 says that you are "*of the same body.*" You belong to a spiritual body that needs you and that you need. I Corinthians 12:12-13 says, "*For as the body is one, and hath many members, and all the members of that one body, being many, are one body: so also is Christ. For by one Spirit are we all baptized into one body, whether we be Jews or Gentiles, whether we be bond or free; and have been all made to drink into one Spirit.*" The body we are "*baptized into,*" or placed into is the church. Ephesians 5:23 teaches that "*Christ is the head of the church: and he is the saviour of the body*" (Ephesians 1:19-23). The local church is the physical gathering of the body of Christ for the purpose of working together for God's glory (Ephesians 3:21). The Apostle Paul explains the purpose of the spiritual leadership of the church and the working together of the members of the church by saying, "*And he gave some, apostles; and some, prophets; and some, evangelists; and some, pastors and teachers; For the perfecting of the saints, for the work of the ministry, for the edifying of the body of Christ: Till we all come in the unity of the faith, and of the knowledge of the Son of God, unto a perfect man, unto the measure of the stature of the fulness of Christ: That we henceforth be no more children, tossed to and fro, and carried about with every wind of doctrine, by the sleight of men, and cunning craftiness, whereby they lie in wait to deceive; But speaking the truth in love, may grow up into him in all things, which is the head, even Christ: From whom the whole body fitly joined together and compacted by that which every joint supplieth, according to the effectual working in the measure of every part, maketh increase of the body unto the edifying of itself in love*" (Ephesians 4:11-16). "*But now hath God set the members every one of them in the body, as it hath pleased him*" (I Corinthians 12:18). "*That there should be no schism in the body; but that the members should have the same care one for another. And whether one member suffer, all the members suffer with it; or one member be honoured, all the members rejoice with it. Now ye are the body of Christ, and members in particular*" (I Corinthians 12:25-27).

Third, Ephesians 3:6 concludes by saying that you are one of the "***partakers of his promise.***" You are a spiritual shareholder in God's promises. You, along with other believers, have a privileged piece of God's greatest promises provided through "***Christ by the Gospel***" (Ephesians 3:6). You have the promise of eternal life (Titus 1:2, I John 2:24-25, II Peter 1:3-4), but you do not have a monopoly on eternal life; you have a partnership with all those who have received His promise by faith in the Gospel as presented in I Corinthians 15:1-4, which says, "***Moreover, brethren, I declare unto you the gospel which I preached unto you, which also ye have received, and wherein ye stand; By which also ye are saved, if ye keep in memory what I preached unto you, unless ye have believed in vain. For I delivered unto you first of all that which I also received, how that Christ died for our sins according to the scriptures; And that he was buried, and that he rose again the third day according to the scriptures.***"

Just as shareholders in a company must work together, fulfilling their personal responsibilities to build the business, and they all patiently wait for their goals to be achieved, so must you fellowship with and serve alongside fellow believers while waiting for God's promises to be fulfilled in your life. The Apostle John desired such fellowship with fellow believers and said, "***That which we have seen and heard declare we unto you, that ye also may have fellowship with us: and truly our fellowship is with the Father, and with his Son Jesus Christ***" (I John 1:3). He was awaiting the same promise that you have today and challenged his readers by saying, "***Let that therefore abide in you, which ye have heard from the beginning. If that which ye have heard from the beginning shall remain in you, ye also shall continue in the Son, and in the Father. And this is the promise that he hath promised us, even eternal life.***" (I John 2:24-25). You have been given the privilege of joining together with other believers to fellowship

Walk in Newness of Life

together as you await the fulfillment of God's blessed promise of eternal life with Him. You are a shareholder with the guarantee of spiritual rewards.

You belong! You have a special and specific place in God the Father's family and have the privilege of living for Him with your brothers and sisters. You also belong in Christ's body, the local church. You need the other members of the body to help you and rejoice with you, and you are needed by them to help them and rejoice with them. And you belong to a special group of shareholders of God's greatest promise of eternal life. You are not alone as you wait for God to fulfill His promise. You have the fellowship of other believers to work alongside you and encourage you as you await for God's perfect fulfillment and your eternal place in glory.

Will you join with your spiritual brothers and sister by meeting with them regularly to encourage them and be encouraged by them? Will you accept the help of and provide help for the other members of Christ's body by participating in your local church? Will you dedicate yourself to working together with fellow shareholder in God's ministry by seeking ways to serve other believers and share God's message of salvation with those around you?

Biblical Instruction about Your New Belonging

- ✓ **Romans 12:3-8** - Each member of the body of Christ has different abilities that God has given to them so that they can help the entire body, and each member should humbly fulfill their responsibility.

- ✓ **I Corinthians 12:12-26** - God has placed each member in the body of Christ to help the church grow and care for itself.

- ✓ **Colossians 2:16, 19** - Jesus Christ is the head of the body, and each member should be unified by receiving their spiritual nourishment from Him.

- ✓ **Galatians 4:1-7** - Each believer is an heir of God as one of His children through their faith in Jesus Christ.

- ✓ **Hebrews 3:6** - Jesus Christ, as the Son of God, is the head of our spiritual family.

- ✓ **I John 5:1-4** - Believers prove their love for their spiritual brothers and sisters when they keep God the Father's commandments.

- ✓ **II John 1:5-8** - Believers should assist their spiritual brothers and sisters as they strive to minister for God the Father.

- ✓ **Philippians 1:3-8** - Believers should be thankful for the fellowship they have together as they serve God together even when they are in different locations.

- ✓ _____ - _____

Walk in Newness of Life

- ✓ _____ - _____
- ✓ _____ - _____
- ✓ _____ - _____
- ✓ _____ - _____
- ✓ _____ - _____
- ✓ _____ - _____
- ✓ _____ - _____
- ✓ _____ - _____
- ✓ _____ - _____
- ✓ _____ - _____
- ✓ _____ - _____

Biblical Investigation about Your New Belonging

Ephesians 3:6

1. In what three ways do you belong now that you are one of God the Father's children?
    - ◆ I am a fellow heir (part of a family)
    - ◆ I am a member in a spiritual body
    - ◆ I am a partaker of God's promise

Romans 8:15-17

2. What Spirit did you receive when you got saved?
   The Spirit of adoption

3. What can you call God now that you are part of His family?
   Abba (daddy)

Ephesians 2:19

4. To whose household do you belong?
   God's

Romans 12:15
Galatians 6:10

5. What should you do with fellows believers who are rejoicing?
   Rejoice

6. What should you do with fellow believers who are weeping?
   Weep

7. What should you do for those who are of the "***household of faith?***"
   Do good

Hebrews 10:24-25

8. What two things should you provoke fellow believers to do?
   ♦ Love
   ♦ Good works

9. What should you not forsake?
   The assembling together of fellow believers

I Corinthians 12:12-27

10. Are each of the members of the Body of Christ (the church) important?
    Yes

11. Who placed you in the Body of Christ (the church) and chosen how you should participate in the ministry?
    God

12. Should there be any schism or division in the Body of Christ (the church)?
    No

13. The members of the Body of Christ (the church) "***should have the same care one for another.***"

14. If one member of the Body of Christ (the church) suffers, all the members should "*suffer*," and if one member is honoured, all the members should "*rejoice*."

Ephesians 1:19-23, 5:23

15. Who is the head of the body (the church)?
    Christ

Ephesians 3:21

16. Who should receive the glory through the ministry of the local church?
    Jesus Christ

Ephesians 3:14-15

17. By Whose family name are you called?
    God the Father's

Ephesians 4:11-16

18. Why has Jesus Christ given spiritual leadership to the body (church)?
    - *For the perfecting of the saints, for the work of the ministry, for the edifying of the body of Christ*
    - *Till we all come in the unity of the faith, and of the knowledge of the Son of God, unto a perfect man, unto the measure of the stature of the fulness of Christ*

- *That we henceforth be no more <u>children</u>, tossed to and fro, and <u>carried</u> about with every wind of doctrine*
- *But <u>speaking</u> the truth in love, may <u>grow</u> up into him in all things*

19. What is the purpose of the body being fitly joined (working) together?
    That the body would edify itself in love

Titus 1:2
I John 2:24-25
II Peter 1:3-4

20. Who promised you eternal life?
    God

I Corinthians 15:1-4

21. What is the Gospel (the good news) that you received and that you should share with others?
    - ***Christ <u>died</u> for our sins according to the scriptures***
    - ***Christ ... was <u>buried</u>***
    - ***Christ ... <u>rose</u> <u>again</u> the third day according to the scriptures***

I John 1:3

22. On Whom is Christian fellowship based?
    - God the Father
    - Jesus Christ

Personal Notes about Your New Belonging

Walk in Newness of Life

Chapter 3

Your New Comforter

John 14:15-17
If ye love me, keep my commandments.
And I will pray the Father,
and he shall give you another Comforter,
that he may abide with you for ever;
Even the Spirit of truth;
whom the world cannot receive,
because it seeth him not, neither knoweth him:
but ye know him;
for he dwelleth with you, and shall be in you.

Chapter 3

Your New Comforter

A Biblical Introduction to Your New Comforter

In John 14:15-17, Jesus Christ makes a promise to His disciples that extends to every believer. He says, "*If ye love me, keep my commandments. And I will pray the Father, and he shall give you another Comforter, that he may abide with you for ever; even the Spirit of truth; whom the world cannot receive, because it seeth him not, neither knoweth him: but ye know him; for he dwelleth with you, and shall be in you.*" Jesus Christ has promised you, as one of His followers, that God the Father will give you a Comforter that will never leave you. That Comforter is the Spirit of Truth, also known as the Holy Spirit. In I Corinthians 3:16, the Apostle Paul teaches about the Holy Spirit's coming by saying, "*Know ye not that ye are the temple of God, and that the Spirit of God dwelleth in you?*" And in I Corinthians 6:19-20, he continues by saying, "*What? know ye not that your body is the temple of the Holy Ghost which is in you, which ye have of God, and ye are not your own? For ye are bought with a price: therefore glorify God in your body, and in your spirit, which are God's.*" God the Father has sent His Comforter, the Holy Spirit, to indwell you, or be with you, at all times, and to guide you through all your Christian life.

God's Comforter, the Holy Spirit, is the Spirit of Truth. Part of the comfort He offers you is His personal guidance in knowing truth (John 14:15-17, 15:26-27, 16:13). In John 15:26, Jesus Christ specifically says, "*But when the Comforter is come, whom I will send unto you from the Father, even the Spirit of truth, which proceedeth from the Father, he shall testify of me.*" In John 16:13, He explains further by saying, "*Howbeit when he, the Spirit of truth, is come, he will guide you into all truth: for he shall not speak of himself; but whatsoever he shall hear, that shall he speak: and he will shew you things to come.*" God has sent His Spirit to comfort you by helping you know His truth for all of life's circumstances, so that you can be spiritually fruitful in all that you do (Galatians 5:22-23, Ephesians 5:9). He desires for you to know the difference between the truth and lies, so He promises to give you spiritual understanding through the Holy Spirit that the world cannot offer you. The Apostle Paul encouraged the believers in I Corinthians 2:12-14, by saying, "*Now we have received, not the spirit of the world, but the spirit which is of God; that we might know the things that are freely given to us of God. Which things also we speak, not in the words which man's wisdom teacheth, but which the Holy Ghost teacheth; comparing spiritual things with spiritual. But the natural man receiveth not the things of the Spirit of God: for they are foolishness unto him: neither can he know them, because they are spiritually discerned.*" God wants you to be comforted by the teaching and understanding that the Holy Spirit offers you as you study and apply the Word of God to your daily life. He does not want you to be confused or discouraged, but rather, confident in what is truth and bold in putting it into practice.

In Romans 8:15-16, the Holy Spirit is called "*the Spirit of adoption,*" and He has been given to you to comfort you with constant reassurance that you are a child of God, and to encourage you to call God the Father "*Abba,*" or "daddy" (Galatians 4:4-7). God, the Father does not want you to go through life insecure. Rather, He wants you to be confidently close to Him so that you are always assured of His love and provision (Hebrews 13:5-6).

Romans 8:26-27 further explains the Holy Spirit's comforting ministry for you during your prayer time as you seek to express your burdens to God but do not know the words to say. It says, "*Likewise the Spirit also helpeth our infirmities: for we know not what we should pray for as we ought: but the Spirit itself maketh intercession for us with groanings which cannot be uttered. And he that searcheth the hearts knoweth what is the mind of the Spirit, because he maketh intercession for the saints according to the will of God.*"

God your Father truly loves you and wants to guide and comfort you through your entire life, for He is *"**the Father of mercies, and the God of all comfort; Who comforteth us in all our tribulation, that we may be able to comfort them which are in any trouble, by the comfort wherewith we ourselves are comforted of God**"* (II Corinthians 1:3-4). He has sent you His personal Comforter, the Holy Spirit, so that you will never need to be alone or confused. Rather, His Comforter desires to work in your life so that you continually grow in your knowledge of and relationship with God the Father and Jesus Christ, which will, in turn produce a life full of spiritual fruit for God's glory.

Will you accept God's Comforter and His ministry to you by following the Holy Spirit's prompting to read, study, and obey God's Word so that you can have His spiritual fruit in your life? Will you also find comfort in the Holy Spirit's ministry of helping you articulate your prayer requests to God the Father?

Biblical Instruction about Your New Comforter

- ✓ **Acts 1:8** - The Holy Spirit has been given to you by God to empower you to be God's witness to those around you.

- ✓ **Acts 2:38-39** - The Holy Spirit was given to you at the moment you believed on Jesus Christ as your personal Savior from your sins.

- ✓ **Ephesians 4:17-32 (30)** - The Holy Spirit can be grieved (saddened) by you if you choose to live in sin, as if you were not saved.

- ✓ **I Thessalonians 5:19** - The Holy Spirit can be quenched (restrained or limit) by you if you choose to not allow Him to fulfill His ministry of teaching you and guiding you to know and live out truth.

- ✓ _____ - _____
- ✓ _____ - _____
- ✓ _____ - _____
- ✓ _____ - _____
- ✓ _____ - _____

Walk in Newness of Life

- ✓ _____ - _____
- ✓ _____ - _____
- ✓ _____ - _____
- ✓ _____ - _____
- ✓ _____ - _____
- ✓ _____ - _____
- ✓ _____ - _____
- ✓ _____ - _____
- ✓ _____ - _____
- ✓ _____ - _____
- ✓ _____ - _____
- ✓ _____ - _____

Biblical Investigation about Your New Comforter

John 14:15-17

1. Who has God the Father promised to give you?
   A Comforter

2. What is another name for the Comforter?
   The Spirit of Truth

3. Does the world have access to God's Comforter?
   No

I Corinthians 3:16

4. Where does the Spirit of Truth (Holy Spirit) dwell?
   In me

I Corinthians 6:19-20

5. Your body is Whose temple?
   The Holy Spirit

John 15:26-27

6. About Whom will the Comforter testify?
   Jesus Christ

John 16:7-13

7. What did Jesus Christ have to do so that the Comforter could come?
   Leave

8. What will the Comforter reprove the world of and why?
   - Sin - They believe not on Jesus Christ
   - Righteousness - Jesus Christ has gone to God the Father to provide righteousness
   - Judgment - The prince of this world is judged

9. What will the Comforter (Spirit of Truth) guide you to know?
   Truth

10. Will the Comforter teach about and glorify Himself?
    No - Jesus Christ

Galatians 5:22-23
Ephesians 5:9

11. What fruit will the Holy Spirit produce in your life?
    - Love
    - Joy
    - Peace
    - Longsuffering
    - Gentleness
    - Goodness
    - Faith
    - Meekness
    - Temperance

Your New Comforter

- ♦ Righteousness
- ♦ Truth

I Corinthians 2:9-14

12. What does the Spirit of God reveal to you?
    The things prepared for us by God

13. Is the Spirit of God also the spirit of the world?
    No

14. How does the Holy Spirit teach?
    Comparing spiritual things with spiritual things

15. Can an unsaved person (natural man) understand spiritual things?
    No

Romans 8:1-17

16. Should you walk after the flesh or after the Spirit?
    After the Spirit

17. Is there condemnation for you when you walk after Spirit of God?
    No

Galatians 4:1-7

18. What does the Spirit of God encourage you to call God? (Galatians 4:1-7)
    Abba (Daddy) Father

Hebrews 13:5-6

19. How long will the "Comforter" be with you?
    Forever

Romans 8:26-27

20. What does the Holy Spirit help you do when you are confused?
    Pray for me

II Corinthians 1:3-4

21. What are the two descriptions of God the Father?
    - Father of mercies
    - God of all comfort

22. In which tribulations does God the Father offer you comfort?
    All

Personal Notes about Your New Comforter

Walk in Newness of Life

Chapter 4

Your New Freedom from Sin

Romans 6:1-2, 6-11
What shall we say then?
Shall we continue in sin, that grace may abound?
God forbid.
How shall we, that are dead to sin, live any longer therein?
Knowing this, that our old man is crucified with him,
that the body of sin might be destroyed,
that henceforth we should not serve sin.
For he that is dead is freed from sin.
Now if we be dead with Christ,
we believe that we shall also live with him:
Knowing that Christ being raised from the dead
dieth no more;
death hath no more dominion over him.
For in that he died, he died unto sin once:
but in that he liveth, he liveth unto God.
Likewise reckon ye also yourselves
to be dead indeed unto sin,
but alive unto God through Jesus Christ our Lord.

Chapter 4

Your New Freedom from Sin

A Biblical Introduction to Your New Freedom from Sin

Romans 6:1 presents an intriguing, yet important question about the new life found in Jesus Christ, as it asks, *"What shall we say then? Shall we continue in sin, that grace may abound?"* It is easy to assume that because Jesus Christ's sacrifice for sin is complete, you now have freedom to sin as often as you choose (Proverbs 28:13, I John 1:9, 2:1-2). But verse 2 provides God's response to man's inquiry by saying, *"God forbid. How shall we, that are dead to sin, live any longer therein?"* Romans chapter six goes on to explain two important spiritual events that take place in your spiritual life at the very moment you accepted Jesus Christ's, death, burial, and resurrection as the only payment for your sin and eternal destiny (Romans 3:23-26, Titus 3:4-7). Galatians 1:4-5, while speaking of Jesus Christ, says, *"Who gave himself for our sins, that he might deliver us from this present evil world, according to the will of God and our Father: To whom be glory for ever and ever. Amen."*

First, Romans 6:6-7 says, *"Knowing this, that our old man is crucified with him, that the body of sin might be destroyed, that henceforth we should not serve sin. For he that is dead is freed from sin."* At the very moment of your faith in Jesus Christ as your personal Savior, God says that you were spiritually placed in Christ and died with Him on the cross so that you could spiritually be *"buried with him ... that like as Christ was raised up from the dead by the glory of the Father, even so we also should walk in newness of life"* (Romans 6:3-4). Colossians 2:12-15 explains that *"ye are risen with him through the faith of the operation of God, who hath*

25

raised him from the dead. And you, being dead in your sins and the uncircumcision of your flesh, hath he quickened together with him, having forgiven you all trespasses; blotting out the handwriting of ordinances that was against us, which was contrary to us, and took it out of the way, nailing it to his cross; and having spoiled principalities and powers, he made a shew of them openly, triumphing over them in it." Although you were not physically with Jesus on the cross, God says that spiritually you died with Him on the cross to free you from sin, and resurrected with Him so that you can have victory over sin as you live for Him (I Corinthians 15:55-58, I John 5:4-5). This truth cannot be observed physically, but is spiritually factual. You are a new creature in Christ, and you have a new opportunity to live a life separated from the power of sin because you died to sin and now can live for God (I Corinthians 5:14-17). So, Romans 6:11-14 plainly says, "*Likewise reckon ye also yourselves to be dead indeed unto sin, but alive unto God through Jesus Christ our Lord. Let not sin therefore reign in your mortal body, that ye should obey it in the lusts thereof. Neither yield ye your members as instruments of unrighteousness unto sin: but yield yourselves unto God, as those that are alive from the dead, and your members as instruments of righteousness unto God. For sin shall not have dominion over you: for ye are not under the law, but under grace. For sin shall not have dominion over you: for ye are not under the law, but under grace.*"

Roman's 6:15 once again asks, "*What then? shall we sin, because we are not under the law, but under grace?*" and then quickly and forcefully says, "*God forbid.*" The Bible is clear that God's forgiving grace should never be taken for granted. "*For the grace of God that bringeth salvation hath appeared to all men, teaching us that, denying ungodliness and worldly lusts, we should live soberly, righteously, and godly, in this present world; looking for that blessed hope, and the glorious appearing of the great God and our Saviour Jesus Christ; Who gave himself for us, that he might redeem us from all iniquity, and purify unto himself a peculiar people, zealous of good works*" (Titus 2:11-14).

Your New Freedom from Sin

Romans 6:16-18 then presents the second spiritual event that took place at your salvation by saying, "*Know ye not, that to whom ye yield yourselves servants to obey, his servants ye are to whom ye obey; whether of sin unto death, or of obedience unto righteousness? But God be thanked, that ye were the servants of sin, but ye have obeyed from the heart that form of doctrine which was delivered you. Being then made free from sin, ye became the servants of righteousness.*" You have been freed from the authority of sin through your relationship with Jesus Christ. Before your salvation, you were sin's slave, and therefore, even your *"righteousnesses are [were] as filthy rags"* (Isaiah 64:6). But Jesus Christ bought you from sin with His blood and has set you free from sin's authority so that you might live to serve your loving Heavenly Father (I Corinthians 6:2, I Peter 1:18-19). And Romans 6:19 encourages you to use your newfound freedom for its intended purpose by saying, "*I speak after the manner of men because of the infirmity of your flesh: for as ye have yielded your members servants to uncleanness and to iniquity unto iniquity; even so now yield your members servants to righteousness unto holiness.*" "*For, brethren, ye have been called unto liberty; only use not liberty for an occasion to the flesh, but by love serve one another. For all the law is fulfilled in one word, even in this; Thou shalt love thy neighbour as thyself*" (Galatians 5:13-14). "*Know ye not, brethren, (for I speak to them that know the law,) how that the law hath dominion over a man as long as he liveth? For the woman which hath an husband is bound by the law to her husband so long as he liveth; but if the husband be dead, she is loosed from the law of her husband. So then if, while her husband liveth, she be married to another man, she shall be called an adulteress: but if her husband be dead, she is free from that law; so that she is no adulteress, though she be married to another man. Wherefore, my brethren, ye also are become dead to the law by the body of Christ; that ye should be married to another, even to him who is raised from the dead, that we should bring forth fruit unto God. For when we were in the flesh, the motions of sins, which were by the law, did work in our members to bring forth fruit unto death. But now we are*

27

Walk in Newness of Life

delivered from the law, that being dead wherein we were held; that we should serve in newness of spirit, and not in the oldness of the letter. Wat shall we say then? Is the law sin? God forbid. Nay, I had not known sin, but by the law: for I had not known lust, except the law had said, Thou shalt not covet" (Romans 7:1-7).

Jesus Christ died on the cross to save you from the power and authority of sin. Through your faith in Him, you are assured access to the spiritual "*victory that overcometh the world*" (I John 5:4). However, it is your daily choice to rely on His resurrection power to resist temptation. You must say with the Apostle Paul, "*I am crucified with Christ: nevertheless I live; yet not I, but Christ liveth in me: and the life which I now live in the flesh I live by the faith of the Son of God, who loved me, and gave himself for me*" (Galatians 2:20). For, "*There hath no temptation taken you but such as is common to man: but God is faithful, who will not suffer you to be tempted above that ye are able; but will with the temptation also make a way to escape, that ye may be able to bear it*" (I Corinthians 10:13).

Will you accept God's freedom from your sin and its shame? Will you enjoy God's power to refuse temptation? Will you take the opportunity God has given you to "*walk in newness of life*" (Romans 6:4)?

Biblical Instruction about Your New Freedom from Sin

- ✓ **Hebrews 2:14-15** - Jesus Christ took on the form of man and died as a man in order to gain victory over death and the Devil.

- ✓ **John 8:34** - Jesus Christ said that a sinner is a servant of his sin.

- ✓ **I John 3:4-6** - Jesus Christ was sent to take away each sinner's sin and prevent him from more sin if he will depend on Him.

- ✓ **Ephesians 2:1-6** - Jesus Christ provides spiritual life to all those who are dead in their sins but are willing to believe in His saving grace.

- ✓ **I Corinthians 6:9-11** - Jesus Christ provides liberty from the power of sin and unrighteousness for all those who believe on His name.

- ✓ _____ - _____

- ✓ _____ - _____

- ✓ _____ - _____

- ✓ _____ - _____

- ✓ _____ - _____

Walk in Newness of Life

- ✓ _____ - _____
- ✓ _____ - _____
- ✓ _____ - _____
- ✓ _____ - _____
- ✓ _____ - _____
- ✓ _____ - _____
- ✓ _____ - _____
- ✓ _____ - _____
- ✓ _____ - _____
- ✓ _____ - _____
- ✓ _____ - _____
- ✓ _____ - _____

Biblical Investigation about Your New Freedom from Sin

Romans 6:1-2, 15

1. Does God want you to continue to sin and depend on His grace for forgiveness?
   No

Proverbs 28:13
I John 1:9-10, 2:1-2

2. How can you have God's forgiveness for your sin?
   Confess my sin

3. What are you if you say that you do not have sin?
   A liar

4. Does God want you to sin?
   No

Romans 3:23-26
Titus 3:4-7

5. Who is the propitiation (payment) for your sin?
   Jesus Christ

Walk in Newness of Life

Galatians 1:3-5

6. When Jesus Christ gave Himself to pay for your sin, from what else did He deliver you?
   <u>The world</u>

7. It is according to Whose will that you are saved from your sin and the world?
   <u>God's</u>

Romans 6:3-14

8. What took place at your salvation?
   - You were <u>baptized</u> into his death
   - You were <u>buried</u> with him by baptism into death
   - You were <u>raised</u> up from the dead

9. What was crucified with Christ at your salvation?
   <u>The old man</u>

10. What should you no longer serve after your salvation?
    <u>Sin</u>

11. For Whom should you live after your salvation?
    <u>God</u>

12. How can you live for God after your salvation?
    11 Likewise <u>reckon</u> ye also yourselves to be <u>dead</u> indeed unto sin, but <u>alive</u> unto God through Jesus Christ our Lord.
    12 Let not sin therefore <u>reign</u> in your mortal body, that ye should <u>obey</u> it in the lusts thereof.

13 Neither <u>yield</u> ye your members as instruments of unrighteousness unto sin: but <u>yield</u> yourselves unto God, as those that are alive from the dead, and your members as instruments of righteousness unto God.
14 For sin shall not have <u>dominion</u> over you: for ye are not under the law, but under grace.

Colossians 2:8-15

13. By what should you not be spoiled?
    - Philosophy
    - Vain deceit
    - Traditions of men
    - Rudiments of the world

14. What took place to you at your salvation?
    12 <u>Buried</u> with him in baptism, wherein also ye are <u>risen</u> with him through the <u>faith</u> of the operation of God, who hath raised him from the dead.
    13 And you, being dead in your sins and the uncircumcision of your flesh, hath he <u>quickened</u> together with him, having <u>forgiven</u> you all trespasses;
    14 Blotting out the handwriting of ordinances that was against us, which was contrary to us, and took it out of the way, <u>nailing</u> it to his cross;
    15 And having <u>spoiled</u> principalities and powers, he made a shew of them openly, <u>triumphing</u> over them in it.

I Corinthians 15:55-58

15. What is the sting of death?
    Sin

Walk in Newness of Life

16. Who gives you victory over death and sin?
    God the Father through Jesus Christ

17. In what should you be steadfast because you have God's promise of victory?
    In the work of the Lord

I John 5:4-5

18. Who overcomes the world?
    The children of God

19. What gives you the guarantee of victory over the world?
    Your faith (in God)

II Corinthians 5:14-17

20. For whom should you live after you have accepted Jesus Christ's love?
    Jesus Christ

21. What happened to you when you accepted Jesus Christ a your personal Savior?
    Created as a new creature

Titus 2:11-14

22. What does God's saving grace teach all men to do while living in this world?
    - Deny <u>ungodliness</u>
    - Deny worldly <u>lusts</u>

Your New Freedom from Sin

- Live <u>soberly</u>
- Live <u>righteously</u>
- Live <u>godly</u>
- Look for that blessed <u>hope</u>, and the glorious <u>appearing</u> of the great God and our Saviour Jesus Christ

23. Why did Jesus Christ give Himself for you?
    - To <u>redeem</u> you from all iniquity
    - To <u>purify</u> you as a peculiar people
    - To make you <u>zealous</u> of good works

Romans 6:16-23

24. Who is your master?
    <u>Whoever you serve</u>

25. From what have you been freed through your faith in Jesus Christ?
    <u>Sin</u>

26. What can you now serve after your faith in Jesus Christ?
    <u>Righteousness</u>

27. What must you do to serve God?
    19 I speak after the manner of men because of the infirmity of your flesh: for as ye have <u>yielded</u> your members servants to <u>uncleanness</u> and to <u>iniquity</u> unto iniquity; even so now <u>yield</u> your members servants to <u>righteousness</u> unto holiness.

28. What is the fruit of serving sin?
    - <u>Shame</u>
    - <u>Death</u>

29. What is the fruit of serving God?
    - Holiness
    - Everlasting life

Isaiah 64:6

30. What is your righteousnesses before your salvation?
    Filthy rages

I Corinthians 6:20
I Peter 1:17-21

31. What price was paid to free you from your sin?
    Jesus' blood

Galatians 5:13-14

32. What should you do with the spiritual freedom Jesus Christ has purchased for you?
    Serve one another

Romans 7:1-7

33. How have you been made dead to the authority of the law and sin?
    Through the death of Jesus Christ

34. For whom should you bring forth fruit in your life of freedom?
    God

Galatians 2:20

35. How did the Apostle Paul want to live his life after his salvation?
20 I am <u>crucified</u> with Christ: nevertheless I <u>live</u>; yet not I, but <u>Christ</u> liveth in me: and the life which I now live in the flesh I live by the <u>faith</u> of the Son of God, who loved me, and gave himself for me.

I Corinthians 10:13

36. Is there any new temptation that will confront you?
   No

37. Will God allow you to be tempted you more than you can resist?
   No

38. What will God provide you with each temptation you confront?
   A way of escape

Personal Notes about
Your New Freedom from Sin

Walk in Newness of Life

Chapter 5

Your New Spiritual Blessing

Ephesians 1:3
Blessed be the God and Father of our Lord Jesus Christ,
who hath blessed us with all spiritual blessings
in heavenly places in Christ:

Chapter 5

Your New Spiritual Blessing

A Biblical Introduction to Your New Spiritual Blessing

Ephesians 1:3 praises God the Father for His overwhelming provision of spiritual blessings for every believer by saying, "***Blessed be the God and Father of our Lord Jesus Christ, who hath blessed us with all spiritual blessings in heavenly places in Christ.***" God has purposefully and carefully planned to bless you in ways that you could never fully understand. The apostle Paul said, "***For I reckon that the sufferings of this present time are not worthy to be compared with the glory which shall be revealed in us***" (Romans 8:18).

God's love for you and His plans to bless you were made "***before the foundation of the world***" and will continue to be fulfilled for all eternity as you live with Him in heaven (Ephesians 1:**4**). He is a loving Father, Who, based on His own will and His own pleasure, predetermined to make available to you the blessing of "***adoption of children by Jesus Christ to himself***" (Ephesians 1:5). After you became His child, He chose from the foundation of the world that you "***should be holy and without blame,***" enjoying His loving presence (Ephesians 1:4).

God was so loving in His plan to bless you that He sent His beloved Son Jesus Christ to offer you "***redemption [from your sins] through his blood, the forgiveness of sins, according to the riches of his grace***" (Ephesians 1:7). He has chosen to abundantly provide "***all [the] wisdom and prudence***" necessary for your life because you have been "***made [you] accepted in the beloved,***" Who is Jesus Christ (Ephesians 1:6, 8).

Walk in Newness of Life

God not only made provision for the forgiveness of your sins, but He also purposefully *"made known unto [you] the mystery of his will"* for your salvation by sending other Christians into your life to present the message of the Gospel, *"how that Christ died for our sins according to the scriptures; and that he was buried, and that he rose again the third day according to the scriptures"* (Ephesians 1:9, I Corinthians 15:1-4). It is this message that you *"trusted, after that ye heard the word of truth, the gospel of your salvation,"* and that has given you the ability to fully enjoy *"all spiritual blessings"* provided for you by God the Father (Ephesians 1:3, 13).

God's desire to bless you has not only given you forgiveness for your sins and a home in heaven, but has also prepared an inheritance for you to enjoy for all eternity (Ephesians 1:11), an inheritance that is *"incorruptible, and undefiled, and that fadeth not away, reserved in heaven for you, who are kept by the power of God through faith unto salvation ready to be revealed in the last time"* (I Peter 1:4-5).

At the moment that you accepted the message of the Gospel, *"ye were sealed with that holy Spirit of promise, which is the ernest of our inheritance"* of great blessings, and *"The Spirit itself beareth witness with our spirit, that we are the children of God: and if children, then heirs; heirs of God"* (Ephesians 1:13-14, Romans 8:14-16). God the Holy Spirit is given to you as a *"Comforter"* and He will *"abide with you for ever"* with the purpose of teaching you about Jesus Christ and God the Father through God's Word the Bible, and to *"guide you into all truth"* (John 14:16-17, 15:26, 16:13-14). Through the work of the Holy Spirit, you can begin to learn more about the *"exceeding great and precious promises"* of blessing that God has planned for you as one of His heirs (Ephesians 1:11, 14, II Peter 1:3-4).

God's plans to continually bless you are extensive. They have been made in love and last for all eternity. Therefore, it is only proper that you would begin living today to the *"to the praise of His glory"* as you will do perfectly in heaven when you are gathered together with all God's children to be in His presence for all eternity (Ephesians 1:10, 12, 14).

Your New Spiritual Blessing

Biblical Instruction about Your New Spiritual Blessing

- ✓ **Matthew 6:19-21, I Corinthians 3:9-15** - Your spiritual inheritance and reward in heaven can be increased as you live for God now.

- ✓ **Matthew 28:18-20, Hebrews 13:5-6** - God has promised the blessing of His presence to those who serve Him.

- ✓ **Luke 12:31-34** - God looks forward to sharing His heavenly kingdom and eternal blessings with you.

- ✓ **Hebrews 10:32-39** - God has promised a great reward of blessing in heaven for those who sacrifice for Him in this life if they are patient.

- ✓ _____ - _____

- ✓ _____ - _____

- ✓ _____ - _____

- ✓ _____ - _____

- ✓ _____ - _____

- ✓ _____ - _____

Walk in Newness of Life

✓ _____ - _____

✓ _____ - _____

✓ _____ - _____

✓ _____ - _____

✓ _____ - _____

✓ _____ - _____

✓ _____ - _____

✓ _____ - _____

✓ _____ - _____

✓ _____ - _____

✓ _____ - _____

✓ _____ - _____

Biblical Investigation about Your New Spiritual Blessing

Ephesians 1:3

1. What has God the Father blessed you with?
   All spiritual blessings

2. Where are your blessings kept secure?
   In Heaven

3. In Whom do you find God's blessings for your life?
   Jesus Christ

Romans 8:18

4. Which is greater?
   ❏ Your current suffering on this earth.
   ❏ God's blessings awaiting you in Heaven.

Ephesians 1:4

5. When did God make His plans to bless you?
   Before the foundation of the world

6. What does God want to help you to become so that you can experience more of His blessings?
   ♦ _Holy_
   ♦ _Without blame_

Ephesians 1:5

7. Who made your spiritual adoption possible?
   Jesus Christ

8. Who is your father when you are spiritually adopted?
   God the Father

Ephesians 1:7

9. What was the price Jesus Christ paid to provide you forgiveness for your sins?
   His blood

I Corinthians 15:1-4

10. What is the Gospel of Jesus Christ?
    3 For I delivered unto you first of all that which I also received, how that Christ died for our sins according to the scriptures;
    4 And that he was buried, and that he rose again the third day according to the scriptures:

Ephesians 1:13

11. What did you do with the Gospel and Jesus Christ in order to guarantee God's blessing?
    Trust (believe) in them

Your New Spiritual Blessing

Ephesians 1:11, 13-14
Romans 8:14-16

12. Who did God give you to assure you of your present and future blessing when you accepted Jesus Christ as your personal Savior?
    The Holy Spirit

13. What blessing does the Holy Spirit guarantee you?
    That I have an inheritance from God the Father

14. Of what does the Holy Spirit assure you?
    That I am a child and heir of God the Father

John 14:16-17, 15:16, 16:13-14

15. What are two other another names for the Holy Spirit?
    - Comforter
    - Spirit of Truth

16. What does the Holy Spirit want to guide you to know?
    All truth

I Peter 1:3-4

17. What are three descriptions of the inheritance God wants to bless you with?
    - Incorruptible
    - Undefiled
    - Fadeth not away

18. Where is your blessed inheritance reserved?
    In Heaven

19. By Whose power are you and your inheritance protected?
    God's

Ephesians 1:10, 12, 14

20. Where will all believers be gathered by God?
    In heaven

21. Who will you praise when you are gathered together with fellow believers in heaven?
    Jesus Christ

22. What spiritual blessing will you fully receive when you are gathered together in heaven with fellow believers?
    Our spiritual inheritance

Personal Notes about Your New Spiritual Blessing

Walk in Newness of Life

Chapter 6

Your New Hope

I Peter 1:3-5
Blessed be the God and Father of our Lord Jesus Christ,
which according to his abundant mercy
hath begotten us again unto a lively hope
by the resurrection of Jesus Christ from the dead,
To an inheritance incorruptible, and undefiled,
and that fadeth not away,
reserved in heaven for you,
Who are kept by the power of God
through faith unto salvation
ready to be revealed in the last time.

Chapter 6

Your New Hope

A Biblical Introduction to Your New Hope

I Peter 1:3-5 praises God the Father for the future hope that He has promised to each believer *"according to his abundant mercy."* You can be assured that God's hope applies to you because ***"of his own will begat he [you] with the word of truth,"*** found in the Gospel of Jesus Christ, which you received to provide you new spiritual life. Because of your new birth and personal relationship with God the Father as one of His children (as studied in Chapter 2), through faith in Jesus Christ, you have been born into or given a birth right of *"**a lively hope.**"*

Your hope, or anticipation and assurance from God, is alive because it is based on the power of ***"the resurrection of Jesus Christ from the dead"*** (I Peter 1:3). It is the power of Jesus Christ's resurrection that has freed you from the power and authority of sin in this life, and it is the power of Jesus Christ's resurrection that assures you of your future eternity with God the Father in heaven (Romans 6). You have the hope or guarantee of ***"an inheritance incorruptible, and undefiled, and that fadeth not away, reserved in heaven for you"*** (I Peter 1:4). Jesus Christ assured His disciples of this hope when He said to them, ***"Let not your heart be troubled: ye believe in God, believe also in me. In my Father's house are many mansions: if it were not so, I would have told you. I go to prepare a place for you. And if I go and prepare a place for you, I will come again, and receive you unto myself; that where I am, there ye may be also"*** (John 14:1-3). The Apostle Paul encourages fellow believers by saying, ***"But I would not have you to be ignorant, brethren, concerning them which are asleep, that ye sorrow not,***

Walk in Newness of Life

even as others which have no hope. For if we believe that Jesus died and rose again, even so them also which sleep in Jesus will God bring with him" (I Thessalonians 4:13-14).

I Peter 1:5 assures you that your new life and your new hope for your eternal future is not based on human power, but "*are kept by the power of God through faith unto salvation ready to be revealed in the last time.*" It is God's power that guaranties your future, and it is your faith in God's salvation through Jesus Christ that makes His power applicable to your life (John 10:27-30). "*For God hath not appointed us to wrath, but to obtain salvation by our Lord Jesus Christ, Who died for us, that, whether we wake or sleep, we should live together with him. Wherefore comfort yourselves together, and edify one another, even as also ye do*" (I Thessalonians 5:9-11).

Your eternal hope is guaranteed to be "*revealed in the last time*" (I Peter 1:5). The "*last time,*" is God's perfect timing for Jesus Christ to "*descend from heaven with a shout, with the voice of the archangel, and with the trump of God: and the dead in Christ shall rise first: then we which are alive and remain shall be caught up together with them in the clouds, to meet the Lord in the air: and so shall we ever be with the Lord*" (I Thessalonians 4:16-18). You must recognize that "*the grace of God that bringeth salvation hath appeared to all men, teaching us that, denying ungodliness and worldly lusts, we should live soberly, righteously, and godly, in this present world; looking for that blessed hope, and the glorious appearing of the great God and our Saviour Jesus Christ; Who gave himself for us, that he might redeem us from all iniquity, and purify unto himself a peculiar people, zealous of good works*" (Titus 2:11-14). "*For we are saved by hope: but hope that is seen is not hope: for what a man seeth, why doth he yet hope for? But if we hope for that we see not, then do we with patience wait for it*" (Romans 8:24-25).

Your new hope is guaranteed by God, and empowered by the resurrection of Jesus Christ. You must "*be sober, putting on the breastplate of faith and love; and for an helmet, the hope of salvation*" (I Thessalonians 5:8). No matter what trials you face in

Your New Hope

this life and the doubts Satan attempts to use to discourage you, you must patiently wait for God's perfect timing, you must maintain your *"hope of eternal life, which God, that cannot lie, promised before the world began"* (Titus 1:2) You must *"gird up the loins of your mind, be sober, and hope to the end for the grace that is to be brought unto you at the revelation of Jesus Christ; as obedient children, not fashioning yourselves according to the former lusts in your ignorance"* (I Peter 1:13-14).

Biblical Instruction about Your New Hope

✓ **Romans 15:13** - God the Father is the resource for you to abound in hope through the ministry of the Holy Spirit in your life.

✓ **I Corinthians 15:12-23, 35-49, 53-58** - The hope of salvation includes the guarantee of resurrection from the dead, just as Jesus Christ was resurrected from the dead.

✓ **Ephesians 2:11-18** - Without a personal relationship with Jesus Christ, there is no hope in this world, nor for eternity, but with Jesus Christ there is abundant hope offered to anyone who will received Him.

✓ **Hebrews 6:17-20** - The hope God offers His children should be a sure anchor for their soul as they face the storms of this life.

✓ **I John 3:1-3** - The hope produced by being one of God's children should produce a desire to live a pure life for His glory.

✓ _____ - _____
_____

✓ _____ - _____
_____

✓ _____ - _____
_____

Walk in Newness of Life

- ✓ _____ - _____
- ✓ _____ - _____
- ✓ _____ - _____
- ✓ _____ - _____
- ✓ _____ - _____
- ✓ _____ - _____
- ✓ _____ - _____
- ✓ _____ - _____
- ✓ _____ - _____
- ✓ _____ - _____
- ✓ _____ - _____
- ✓ _____ - _____

Biblical Investigation about Your New Hope

I Peter 1:3-5

1. Who has provided new hope for your life?
   <u>God the Father</u>

2. What is the description given about your new hope?
   <u>Lively</u>

3. What type of inheritance are you hoping for?
   - <u>Incorruptible</u>
   - <u>Undefiled</u>
   - <u>Fadeth not away</u>
   - <u>Reserved in heaven</u>

4. Whose power guarantees you your new hope following your faith in Jesus Christ?
   <u>God the Father's</u>

James 1:17-18

5. By Whose will were you were saved (spiritually begotten)?
   <u>God the Father's</u>

John 14:1-3

6. Where has Jesus Christ promised to take you to be with Him?
   <u>Heaven</u>

I Thessalonians 4:13-14

7. Should you sorrow without hope when a fellow believer passes away?
   No

8. Why should you have hope when a believer passes away?
   Because they will be raised again like Jesus

John 10:27-30

9. After you have received your hope of eternal life through Jesus Christ, can anyone take you out of God's hands?
   No

I Thessalonians 4:16-18, 5:9-11

10. What should you do with other believers because of your hope of salvation and future ascension to heaven to be with Jesus Christ?
    ♦ Comfort them
    ♦ Edify them

Titus 2:11-14

11. What type of hope do you have through your salvation?
    Blessed

12. What should your hope help you look forward to?
    The coming of Jesus Christ

Your New Hope

13. Who gave Himself so that you can have spiritual hope?
    Jesus Christ

Romans 8:24-25

14. Is hope something you can see or touch?
    No

15. What must you do while you hope for your final salvation from this world?
    Wait patiently

I Thessalonians 5:8
Ephesians 6:17

16. What area of your spiritual body does your hope of salvation protect?
    Head (mind and thinking)

Titus 1:2

17. Who promised your hope of salvation to you?
    God the Father

18. Can the promise of your salvation ever fail?
    No

I Peter 1:13-14

19. Until when should you be sober and hope for the grace of God through Jesus Christ?
    Until the end

20. How should you live based on your hope in God's grace?
    As an obedient child - not in lust and ignorance

Personal Notes about Your New Hope

Walk in Newness of Life

Chapter 7

Your New Focus

Colossians 3:1-2
If ye then be risen with Christ,
seek those things which are above,
where Christ sitteth on the right hand of God.
Set your affection on things above,
not on things on the earth.

Chapter 7

Your New Focus

A Biblical Introduction to Your New Focus

Colossians 3:1-2 builds on your new hope found in Jesus Christ's resurrection from the dead, which was considered in chapter 6, *"If ye then be risen with Christ, seek those things which are above, where Christ sitteth on the right hand of God. Set your affection on things above, not on things on the earth."* The Apostle John wrote in I John 2:15-17, *"Love not the world, neither the things that are in the world. If any man love the world, the love of the Father is not in him. For all that is in the world, the lust of the flesh, and the lust of the eyes, and the pride of life, is not of the Father, but is of the world. And the world passeth away, and the lust thereof: but he that doeth the will of God abideth for ever."*

In Colossians 2:10-15, the Apostle Paul boldly declares your spiritual victory over sin and death through Jesus Christ by saying, *"And ye are complete in [Christ], which is the head of all principality and power: ... Buried with him in baptism, wherein also ye are risen with him through the faith of the operation of God, who hath raised him from the dead. And you, being dead in your sins and the uncircumcision of your flesh, hath he quickened together with him, having forgiven you all trespasses; blotting out the handwriting of ordinances that was against us, which was contrary to us, and took it out of the way, nailing it to his cross; and having spoiled principalities and powers, he made a shew of them openly, triumphing over them in it."* Although you may not physically feel any different, spiritually you have experienced a supernatural transformation when you accepted Jesus Christ as your personal Savior. At that very moment you were spiritually *"baptized*

Walk in Newness of Life

*into [Jesus Christ's] death. Therefore [you were] **buried with him by baptism into death: that like as Christ was raised up from the dead by the glory of the Father, even so [you] also should walk in newness of life***" (Romans 6:3-4)

Your new life now allows you to enjoy a new focus and goals. You have the opportunity to seek after something better than this world can offer you and to depend on someone who will never fail you. You can now invest in heavenly treasures with eternal value by placing your loving attention on God and what truly glorifies and exalts Him (Matthew 22:36-40).

Jesus Christ said, "***Lay not up for yourselves treasures upon earth, where moth and rust doth corrupt, and where thieves break through and steal: but lay up for yourselves treasures in heaven, where neither moth nor rust doth corrupt, and where thieves do not break through nor steal: For where your treasure is, there will your heart be also***" (Matthew 6:19-21). In I Corinthians 9:25-27, the Apostle Paul said, "***And every man that striveth for the mastery is temperate in all things. Now they do it to obtain a corruptible crown; but we an incorruptible. I therefore so run, not as uncertainly; so fight I, not as one that beateth the air.***" "***I press toward the mark for the prize of the high calling of God in Christ Jesus***" (Philippians 3:14). Paul did not want to take the chance of losing his heavenly focus. He did not want to lose any spiritual treasures that he could gain by properly living for and serving His Lord and Savior Jesus Christ in this life. At the end of his life, he said, "***I have fought a good fight, I have finished my course, I have kept the faith: henceforth there is laid up for me a crown of righteousness, which the Lord, the righteous judge, shall give me at that day: and not to me only, but unto all them also that love his appearing***" (II Timothy 4:7-8). You have the opportunity to win a crown of righteousness in heaven if you will focus your life on heavenly things.

You must "***lay aside every weight, and the sin which doth so easily beset us, and let us run with patience the race that is set before us, looking unto Jesus the author and finisher of our faith; who for the joy that was set before him endured the cross,***

48

Your New Focus

despising the shame, and is set down at the right hand of the throne of God. For consider him that endured such contradiction of sinners against himself, lest ye be wearied and faint in your minds" (Hebrews 12:1-3). You must dedicate yourself to personally and regularly study God's Word so that you might, with the help of the Holy Spirit, continually grow in your knowledge of God the Father and Jesus Christ and obedience to what glorifies Them. By doing so, you will truly enjoy the heavenly rewards God has awaiting for you. As you seek God's glory and love Him, you will find that the things of this world, although necessary for living, are not necessary for a fulfilled life, and you will experience God's "*Grace and peace be[ing] multiplied unto you through the knowledge of God, and of Jesus our Lord, according as his divine power hath given unto us all things that pertain unto life and godliness, through the knowledge of him that hath called us to glory and virtue*" (II Peter 1:2-3).

Biblical Instruction about Your New Focus

✓ **Matthew 6:25-34** - When a believer focuses on heaven and living according to God's righteousness, he has God's promise to provide for his earthly needs.

✓ **Matthew 7:7-8** - Each believer has God's promise that he will reveal Himself, if he seek Him.

✓ **II Corinthians 4:18** - Each believer must seek eternal things, rather than the things of this world.

✓ **I Corinthians 10:31** - Each believer must seek God's glory in everything he does.

✓ _____ - _____

✓ _____ - _____

✓ _____ - _____

✓ _____ - _____

✓ _____ - _____

✓ _____ - _____

Walk in Newness of Life

- ✓ _____ - _____
- ✓ _____ - _____
- ✓ _____ - _____
- ✓ _____ - _____
- ✓ _____ - _____
- ✓ _____ - _____
- ✓ _____ - _____
- ✓ _____ - _____
- ✓ _____ - _____
- ✓ _____ - _____
- ✓ _____ - _____
- ✓ _____ - _____

Your New Focus

Biblical Investigation about Your New Focus

Colossians 3:1-2

1. What should you seek after if you are a follower of Jesus Christ?
   Things above

2. Where should you set your affections if you are follower of Jesus Christ?
   Things above

3. Where should you not set your affections if you are a follower of Jesus Christ?
   Things on the earth

I John 2:15-17

4. Can you set your affections on God and on worldly objects and philosophies at the same time?
   No

5. What three things are included in a worldly focus?
   - Lust of the flesh
   - Lust of the eyes
   - Pride of life

6. What will take place with this world and those who focus on it?
   They will pass away

Walk in Newness of Life

7. What will take place with those who put their focus on pleasing God?
   They will abide forever

Colossians 2:10-15

8. Who has provided you victory over your sin?
   Jesus Christ

9. Where was your sin placed when you accepted Jesus Christ as your personal Savior?
   The cross

Romans 6:3-4

10. With whose death, burial and resurrection were you identified at your salvation?
    Jesus Christ's

11. How should you now walk following your salvation?
    In newness of life

Matthew 22:36-40

12. What is the first great commandment, and how should you fulfill it?
    Love the Lord your God - with all our life

13. What is the second great commandment, and how should you fulfill it?
    Love my neighbour - as myself

Your New Focus

Matthew 6:19-21

14. Where should you not lay up your treasure, and why?
    On earth - they will get ruined

15. Where should you lay up your treasure and why?
    In Heaven - they can not be ruined

16. What does your treasure reveal about you?
    My heart's focus

I Corinthians 9:25-27

17. What type of crown did the Apostle Paul desire to win?
    Incorruptible

18. How did the Apostle Paul not run the race of his life?
    Uncertainly (without control)

19. How did the Apostle Paul not fight his spiritual battles?
    Beating the air (without focus on a target)

Philippians 3:14

20. What mark did the Apostle Paul set his sights on so that he would not fail in his Christian life?
    The prize of the high calling of God in Jesus

II Timothy 4:7-8

21. Why was the Apostle Paul sure he would receive a crown of righteousness when he arrived in heaven?
    7 I have <u>fought</u> a good fight, I have <u>finished</u> my course, I have <u>kept</u> the faith:

22. How can you earn a crown of righteousness when you get to heaven?
    love (be ready for) Jesus Christ's coming

Hebrews 12:1-3

23. What must you lay aside so that you can properly focus on your Christian life?
    - Any weight (distraction)
    - Any sin

24. How must you run the Christian race so that you finish well?
    With patience

25. On Whom must you focus so that you do not become discouraged in your Christian life?
    Jesus Christ

II Peter 1:2-4

26. How can you have the grace and peace you need to live your Christian life?
    By knowing God the Father and Jesus Christ

Your New Focus

27. On Whom must you focus if you are to you have all that you need to live a godly life?
    - ♦ God the Father
    - ♦ Jesus Christ

Personal Notes about Your New Focus

Walk in Newness of Life

Chapter 8

Your New Mind

Romans 12:2
And be not conformed to this world:
but be ye transformed by the renewing of your mind,
that ye may prove what is that good,
and acceptable, and perfect, will of God.

Chapter 8

Your New Mind

A Biblical Introduction to Your New Mind

Romans 12:2 presents the first step you must take in order for you to live your new life in Christ when it says, *"**And be not conformed to this world: but be ye transformed by the renewing of your mind, that ye may prove what is that good, and acceptable, and perfect, will of God.**"* You must allow God to renew or renovate your way of thinking so that you can truly fulfill His will for your life. His will is good, acceptable and perfect for you in every way imaginable!

Earlier in Romans 7:22-23, when the Apostle Paul was sharing his own spiritual battle with his flesh, he said, *"**For I delight in the law of God after the inward man: but I see another law in my members, warring against the law of my mind, and bringing me into captivity to the law of sin which is in my members.**"* In these verses, the Apostle Paul expressed the spiritual struggle that each believer faces as their mind becomes a spiritual battle ground, for it is the mind that *"**the fiery darts of the wicked**"* targets, it is on the mind that the world focuses its temptations through *"**the lust of the flesh, and the lust of the eyes, and the pride of life,**"* and it is the mind where one's own flesh fights to bring them *"**into captivity to the law of sin**"* (Ephesians 6:16, Juan 2:16, Romans 7:23). The Apostle Paul concludes in verses 24-25 by saying, *"**O wretched man that I am! who shall deliver me from the body of this death? I thank God through Jesus Christ our Lord. So then with the mind I myself serve the law of God; but with the flesh the law of sin**"* (Romans 7:24-25). Here, Apostle Paul reveals the only solution available for renewing your mind. You must begin, and never stop,

Walk in Newness of Life

"*Looking unto Jesus the author and finisher of our faith*" by learning and remembering the "*law of God,*" the Bible, "*lest ye be wearied and faint in your minds*" (Hebrews 12:2-3). You must follow the Apostle Paul's counsel to Timothy when he said, "*Meditate upon these things; give thyself wholly to them; that thy profiting may appear to all. Take heed unto thyself, and unto the doctrine; continue in them: for in doing this thou shalt both save thyself, and them that hear thee*" (I Timothy 4:15-16). You must heed the Apostle Paul's warning to not permit Satan to distract you from Jesus Christ, which is found in II Corinthians 11:3, "*But I fear, lest by any means, as the serpent beguiled Eve through his subtilty, so your minds should be corrupted from the simplicity that is in Christ.*"

Romans 8:5-7 distinguishes between those who permit the Holy Spirit to guide their mind through reading, understanding, and remembering God's Word so that they can put it into practice, and those who permit their flesh to dictate their thoughts and actions. It says, "*For they that are after the flesh do mind the things of the flesh; but they that are after the Spirit the things of the Spirit. For to be carnally minded is death; but to be spiritually minded is life and peace. Because the carnal mind is enmity against God: for it is not subject to the law of God, neither indeed can be. So then they that are in the flesh cannot please God.*" The "*carnal mind*" thinks about those things that please self, and therefore, produce a life full of "*the works of the flesh ... which are these; Adultery, fornication, uncleanness, lasciviousness, idolatry, witchcraft, hatred, variance, emulations, wrath, strife, seditions, heresies, envyings, murders, drunkenness, revellings, and such like*" (Galatians 5:19-21). "*Among whom also we all had our conversation in times past in the lusts of our flesh, fulfilling the desires of the flesh and of the mind; and were by nature the children of wrath, even as others. But God, who is rich in mercy, for his great love wherewith he loved us, even when we were dead in sins, hath quickened us together with Christ, (by grace ye are saved;)*" (Ephesians 2:3-5). Although you were born with a "*carnal mind,*" God, through His salvation in Jesus Christ, has provided you

Your New Mind

the opportunity to renovate your mind so that you can *"**be spiritually minded**"* and enjoy you new *"**life and peace**"* (Romans 8:6). Following your salvation, you are commanded *"**that ye henceforth walk not as other Gentiles walk, in the vanity of their mind, having the understanding darkened, being alienated from the life of God through the ignorance that is in them, because of the blindness of their heart ... But ye have not so learned Christ ... be renewed in the spirit of your mind; And that ye put on the new man, which after God is created in righteousness and true holiness.**"* (Ephesians 4:17-24). Your salvation does not only save you from the penalty of sin, but also provides you instructions to change your way of thinking, which will then keep you from continuing to live in sin. Titus 2:11-14 says, *"**For the grace of God that bringeth salvation hath appeared to all men, teaching us that, denying ungodliness and worldly lusts, we should live soberly, righteously, and godly, in this present world; Looking for that blessed hope, and the glorious appearing of the great God and our Saviour Jesus Christ; Who gave himself for us, that he might redeem us from all iniquity, and purify unto himself a peculiar people, zealous of good works.**"*

The process of any renovation project is not easy or quick. It requires dedicated labor to remove the old and replace it with something new. It is not sufficient to cover up the old with the new, or to mix new things with old things. Spiritually, you must begin by humbly accepting that your old thoughts and desires are contrary to God's, and therefore, need to be removed so you can begin to learn His thoughts and desires for your life. You must recognize you are not sufficient enough to fulfill this renovation process by yourself, and you must obey God's command found in Romans 12:3, *"**not to think of himself [yourself] more highly than he [you] ought to think; but to think soberly, according as God hath dealt to every man the measure of faith**"* (Galatians 6:3). You must ask God to teach you His mind through the direction of the Spirit of Truth, the Holy Spirit, which has been given to you by God to *"**guide you into all truth**"* (John 16:13). And then you must receive *"**the word [of God] with all readiness of mind, and searched the scriptures**"*

57

Walk in Newness of Life

daily," so that you can continually discover what God says is true about your life and how you can live for Him (Acts 17:11).

It is only by God's guidance through His Word that you can truly begin to transform your mind into "***the mind of Christ***" (I Corinthians 2:9-16). Christ's mind was one of humility, service, and love for God the Father and others (Philippians 2:2-8). This is the same mind, or thinking, that will guide you to fulfill God's stated will for your life, that you "***love the Lord thy God with all thy heart, and with all thy soul, and with all thy mind,***" and that you "***love thy neighbour as thyself***" (Matthew 22:37-39).

The renovation process will require you to "***gird up the loins of your mind, be sober, and hope to the end for the grace that is to be brought unto you at the revelation of Jesus Christ; as obedient children, not fashioning yourselves according to the former lusts in your ignorance***" (I Peter 1:13-15). You must be willing to ask the question found in Psalm 119:9, which says, "***Wherewithal shall a young man cleanse his way?***" and then follow the answer provided, "***by taking heed thereto according to thy word.***" You must follow the six steps found in Psalm 119:10-14 to permit God's Word to penetrate every area of your life. First, you must seek God's Word with your whole heart. Second, you must never wander from God's Word. Third, you must hide or keep God's Word close to your heart and thoughts. Fourth, you must allow God to teach you the meaning and personal application of His Word. Fifth, you must confidently share what you have learned from God's Word with those around you. Sixth, you must rejoice in the direction God's Word has take you life. By following the six steps found in Psalm 119:10-14 to every area of your daily private and public life, you will naturally begin to fulfill verses 15-16 as you meditate, have respect unto, delight, and not forget God's Word on a regular basis. Through these God-given steps, you will find yourself saying with King David in Psalm 19:7-11, "***The law of the LORD is perfect, converting the soul: the testimony of the LORD is sure, making wise the simple. The statutes of the LORD are right, rejoicing the heart: the commandment of the LORD is pure, enlightening the eyes. The fear of the LORD is clean, enduring for ever: the judgments of the***

Your New Mind

LORD are true and righteous altogether. More to be desired are they than gold, yea, than much fine gold: sweeter also than honey and the honeycomb. Moreover by them is thy servant warned: and in keeping of them there is great reward." "*For the word of God is quick, and powerful, and sharper than any twoedged sword, piercing even to the dividing asunder of soul and spirit, and of the joints and marrow, and is a discerner of the thoughts and intents of the heart"* (Hebrews 4:12).

You must take control of your own thoughts, and obey Philippians 4:8, which says, "*Finally, brethren, whatsoever things are true, whatsoever things are honest, whatsoever things are just, whatsoever things are pure, whatsoever things are lovely, whatsoever things are of good report; if there be any virtue, and if there be any praise, think on these things.*" The Bible is very clear when it says, "*For as [a man] thinketh in his heart, so is he*" (Proverbs 23:7). Your thoughts today will turn into actions tomorrow. Therefore, you must take charge of your thoughts and purposefully reject those thoughts, temptations, desires, etc., that are contrary to God's Word and are not verifiable reality. In order to do this, you must allow God to renew, or renovate, your way of thinking by "*meditating*" or concentrating, on His Word "*day and night, that thou mayest observe to do according to all that is written therein: for then thou shalt make thy way prosperous, and then thou shalt have good success*" (Joshua 1:8). For "*Blessed is the man*" whose "*delight is in the law of the LORD; and in his law doeth he meditate day and night. And [you] shall be like a tree planted by the rivers of water, that bringeth forth [your] fruit in his season; [your] leaf also shall not wither; and whatsoever [you] doeth shall prosper*" (Psalm 1:1-3).

There is no thought that is hidden from God or that will not affect your life (Ecclesiastes 12:13-14). You must not be carnally minded, "*For to be carnally minded is death; but to be spiritually minded is life and peace.*" (Romans 8:5-8). You must seek God's help in changing your mind to be like His, to think His thoughts, and understand things from His perspective (James 1:5-8). You must say with the Psalmist, "*O how love I thy law! it is my meditation all the*

59

Walk in Newness of Life

day," and recognize that you can have "***more understanding than all [your] teachers***" when God's "***testimonies are [your] meditations***" (Psalm 119:97, 99).

Biblical Instruction about Your New Mind

✓ **Isaiah 26:3-4** - Each believer can find perfect peace in their life as they keep their mind thinking on and trusting in God.

✓ **Romans 6:11-13** - Each believer must believe themselves to be dead to sin and alive to live for God through Jesus Christ.

✓ **Romans 12:16** - Each believer must seek to be in agreement with fellow believers by being humbly minded.

✓ **Philippians 4:6-7** - Each believer can enjoy peace of mind as they take their requests to God in prayer.

✓ **Colossians 3:5-10** - Each believer must recognize that their way of thinking before they were saved must be eliminated, and that they must begin to renew their thinking by growing in their knowledge of Jesus Christ.

✓ **I Peter 4:1-3** - Each believer must have the mind of Jesus Christ in separating themself from the sin of the flesh.

✓ _____ - _____

✓ _____ - _____

✓ _____ - _____

✓ _____ - _____

Walk in Newness of Life

- ✓ _____ - _____
- ✓ _____ - _____
- ✓ _____ - _____
- ✓ _____ - _____
- ✓ _____ - _____
- ✓ _____ - _____
- ✓ _____ - _____
- ✓ _____ - _____
- ✓ _____ - _____
- ✓ _____ - _____
- ✓ _____ - _____
- ✓ _____ - _____

Biblical Investigation about Your New Mind

Romans 12:2

1. What is required so that you are not conformed to this world?
   Your mind must be transformed - renewed

Romans 7:22-25

2. Where does the law of sin battle you?
   In your mind

3. Who can deliver you from the law of sin?
   God through Jesus Christ

Hebrews 12:2-3

4. To Whom must you look so that you do not faint in your mind?
   Jesus Christ - the Author and Finisher of the our faith

I Timothy 4:15-16

5. What must you do with God's doctrine (teaching) so that you may save yourself and those who will hear you?
   - Meditate on them
   - Give myself wholly to them

Walk in Newness of Life

II Corinthians 11:3

6. From what must you guard your mind from being corrupted (distracted)?
   The simplicity of Jesus Christ

Romans 8:5-8

7. Who is the carnal mind enmity against?
   God

8. Can you please God if your mind is carnal?
   No

Galatians 5:19-21

9. Can those who are not saved from a carnal mind and fleshly sins inherit the kingdom of God?
   NO

Ephesians 2:3-5

10. Before your salvation, what did you fulfill?
    - The desires of the flesh
    - The desires of the mind

Ephesians 4:17-24

11. How do the unsaved walk?
    In the vanity of their mind

Your New Mind

12. From Whom must you learn so that you can be freed from your old mind?
    Jesus Christ

13. What must you renew so that you can put on the new man?
    My mind

Titus 2:11-14

14. What does the grace of salvation teach you?
    11 For the grace of God that bringeth salvation hath appeared to all men,
    12 Teaching us that, denying <u>ungodliness</u> and worldly <u>lusts</u>, we should live <u>soberly</u>, <u>righteously</u>, and <u>godly</u>, in this present world;
    13 Looking for that blessed <u>hope</u>, and the glorious <u>appearing</u> of the great God and our Saviour Jesus Christ;
    14 Who gave himself for us, that he might <u>redeem</u> us from all iniquity, and <u>purify</u> unto himself a peculiar people, zealous of good works.

Galatians 6:3

15. Who do you deceive if you think yourself to be something that you are not?
    Myself

Romans 12:3

16. How must you think about yourself?
    Soberly

John 16:13

17. What does the Holy Spirit want to teach you?
    Truth

Acts 17:11

18. What type of mind must you have as you study God's Word?
    A ready mind

I Corinthians 2:9-16

19. Whose mind do you have through the Holy Spirit?
    Jesus Christ's

Philippians 2:2-8

20. What type of mind must you have if you are to be like-minded with fellow believers?
    Lowly minded

21. Who is the example of being lowly minded?
    Jesus Christ

Matthew 22:37-39

22. How should you love the Lord your God?
    37 Jesus said unto him, Thou shalt love the Lord thy God with all thy heart, and with all thy soul, and with <u>all</u> thy mind.

Your New Mind

I Peter 1:13-15

23. What must you do with the loins of your mind so that you can think soberly?
    <u>Gird up its loins</u>

Psalm 119:9-14

24. What must you heed in order to cleanse your ways?
    <u>God's Word</u>

25. What must you do with God's Word so that it can cleanse your ways?

    10 With my whole heart have I <u>sought</u> thee: O let me not <u>wander</u> from thy commandments.
    11 Thy word have I <u>hid</u> in mine heart, that I might not sin against thee.
    12 Blessed art thou, O LORD: <u>teach</u> me thy statutes.
    13 With my lips have I <u>declared</u> all the judgments of thy mouth.
    14 I have <u>rejoiced</u> in the way of thy testimonies, as much as in all riches.
    15 I will <u>meditate</u> in thy precepts, and have <u>respect</u> unto thy ways.
    16 I will <u>delight</u> myself in thy statutes: I will not <u>forget</u> thy word.

Psalm 19:7-11

26. What is perfect and converts the soul?
    <u>The law of the Lord</u>

27. What is sure and makes the simple wise?
    <u>The testimony of the Lord</u>

Walk in Newness of Life

28. What is right and rejoices the heart?
    The statutes of the Lord

29. What is pure and enlightens the eyes?
    The commandments of the Lord

30. What is clean and endures forever?
    The fear of the Lord

31. What is true and righteous altogether?
    The judgments of the Lord

32. What should you desire more than gold?
    The judgments of the Lord

33. What is sweeter than honey?
    The judgments of the Lord

34. What warns God's servant?
    The judgments of the Lord

35. What brings great reward when they are kept?
    The judgments of the Lord

Hebrews 4:12

36. What is God's Word is described as being?
    - Quick (alive)
    - Powerful
    - Sharper than any twoedged sword

37. What does God's Word discern?
    - Thoughts
    - Intents of the heart

Philippians 4:8

38. On what should you think?
    8 Finally, brethren, whatsoever things are <u>true</u>, whatsoever things are <u>honest</u>, whatsoever things are <u>just</u>, whatsoever things are <u>pure</u>, whatsoever things are <u>lovely</u>, whatsoever things are of <u>good</u> report; if there be any virtue, and if there be any praise, think on these things.

Proverbs 23:7

39. What determines who you are?
    What you think in your heart

Joshua 1:8

40. On what should you meditate?
    The book of the law (God's Word)

41. What is the reward for observing what God's Word says?
    - A prosperous way
    - Good success

Psalm 1:1-3

42. How often should you meditate on God's Word?
    <u>Day and night</u>

Ecclesiastes 12:13-14

43. What is your duty?
    13 Let us hear the conclusion of the whole matter: <u>Fear</u> God, and <u>keep</u> his commandments: for this is the whole duty of man.

44. Will God judge you for secret things?
    <u>Yes</u>

James 1:5-8

45. What must you do to receive wisdom from God?
    <u>Ask in faith</u>

Psalm 119:97

46. If you love God's Word, how long will you meditate on it?
    <u>All day</u>

Psalm 1119:99

47. What will be the result of meditating on God's Word?
    <u>I will have more understanting than my teachers</u>

Personal Notes about Your New Mind

Walk in Newness of Life

Chapter 9

Your New Spiritual Hunger

I Peter 2:1-3
Wherefore laying aside all malice, and all guile,
and hypocrisies, and envies, and all evil speakings,
As newborn babes,
desire the sincere milk of the word,
that ye may grow thereby:
If so be ye have tasted that the Lord is gracious.

Chapter 9

Your New Spiritual Hunger

A Biblical Introduction about Your Spiritual New Hunger

I Peter 2:1-3 explains the importance of God's Word being a part of each new believer's spiritual life. It begins by commanding each believer to be *"laying aside all malice, and all guile, and hypocrisies, and envies, and all evil speakings."* Then it explains the process by which such a command can be accomplished by saying *"as newborn babes, desire the sincere milk of the word, that ye may grow thereby."* And it concludes by providing the motivation for allowing God's Word to change their life when it says, *"if so be ye have tasted that the Lord is gracious."*

At your salvation, you were born again to a new spiritual life through the finished work of Jesus Christ (Romans 6:4). Now you have the responsibility to spiritually mature through partaking of the spiritual nourishment of God's Word. Just as a baby hungers for milk, and grows the more he enjoys it's nourishment, so you will grow spiritually as you enjoy reading, meditating on, and living God's Word. And as you grow, you will begin to be able to enjoy not just the milk of the Word (basic truths about sin, salvation, etc.) but also the meat of the Word (profound truths about God, Christian living, etc.), so that through your greater understanding you will be able to gain spiritual discernment of good and evil (Hebrews 5:12-13).

The apostle Paul, knowing the importance of God's Word for salvation, as well as for a mature Christian life, said to Timothy *"continue thou in the things which thou hast learned and hast been assured of, knowing of whom thou hast learned them; and that from a child thou hast known the holy scriptures, which are*

Walk in Newness of Life

able to make thee wise unto salvation through faith which" (II Timothy 3:14-15). God's Word was sufficient to reveal salvation to Timothy and It was sufficient to show Timothy how to live following his salvation. For "*all scripture is given by inspiration of God, and is profitable for doctrine, for reproof, for correction, for instruction in righteousness: that the man of God may be perfect, throughly furnished unto all good works*" (II Timothy 3:16-17).

It is God's plan to bless you in your new life, however you must choose to follow the pattern given in Psalm 1:1-3 which says, "*Blessed is the man that walketh not in the counsel of the ungodly, nor standeth in the way of sinners, nor sitteth in the seat of the scornful. But his delight is in the law of the LORD; and in his law doth he meditate day and night. And he shall be like a tree planted by the rivers of water, that bringeth forth his fruit in his season; his leaf also shall not wither; and whatsoever he doeth shall prosper.*" You must daily choose to reject the philosophies and life styles of this world and to meditate and apply God's Word in every area of your life. You must obey God's command given to all believers to "*lay apart all filthiness and superfluity of naughtiness, and receive with meekness the engrafted word, which is able to save your souls. But be ye doers of the word, and not hearers only, deceiving your own selves. For if any be a hearer of the word, and not a doer, he is like unto a man beholding his natural face in a glass: for he beholdeth himself, and goeth his way, and straightway forgetteth what manner of man he was. But whoso looketh into the perfect law of liberty, and continueth therein, he being not a forgetful hearer, but a doer of the work, this man shall be blessed in his deed*" (James 1:21-25).

Because you "*have tasted that the Lord is gracious,*" through the message of salvation found in the Bible, you should naturally have an appetite to learn more about God and His will for your life which can only be satisfied by reading more of and thinking on His Word (I Peter 2:3). You must say with the Psalmist "*The law of thy mouth is better unto me than thousands of gold and silver,*" "*Thy word is very pure: therefore they servant loveth it*" (Psalm 119:72, 140). Then will you learn to say with King David "*The law of the*

Your New Spiritual Hunger

LORD is perfect, converting the soul: The testimony of the LORD is sure, making wise the simple. The statutes of the LORD are right, rejoicing the heart: The commandment of the LORD is pure, enlightening the eyes. The fear of the LORD is clean, enduring for ever: The judgments of the LORD are true and righteous altogether. More to be desired are they than gold, yea, than much fine gold: Sweeter also than honey and the honeycomb. Moreover by them is thy servant warned: And in keeping of them there is great reward" (Psalm 19:7-11). "*O God, thou art my God; early will I seek thee: my soul thirsteth for thee, my flesh longeth for thee in a dry and thirsty land, where no water is; to see thy power and thy glory, so as I have seen thee in the sanctuary. When I remember thee upon my bed, and meditate on thee in the night watches. Because thou hast been my help, therefore in the shadow of thy wings will I rejoice*" (Psalm 63:1-2, 6-7).

You must chose to follow the example of the new believers in Berea who, "*received the word with all readiness of mind, and searched the scriptures daily, whether those things were so.*" (Acts 17:10-11). You must purposefully set aside time each day to read, study, memorize, and share with others the very book that has changed your life, God's Word, the Bible (II Timothy 2:15).

Your New Spiritual Hunger

Biblical Instruction about Your New Spiritual Hunger

✓ **Deuteronomy 6:4-19** - God's Word should be displayed, talked about, and taught from one generation to another.

✓ **Romans 10:17** - God's Word must be listened to in order for faith to grow.

✓ **I Corinthians 3:1-3** - The meat of God's Word cannot be received by carnal Christians.

✓ **II Peter 1:16-21** - God's Word can always be trusted and is for all people to read and study.

✓ **Hebrews 4:12** - God's Word is alive and penetrates to the very soul of man.

✓ _____ - _____

✓ _____ - _____

✓ _____, _____ - _____

✓ _____ - _____

✓ _____ - _____

Walk in Newness of Life

- ✓ _____ - _____
- ✓ _____ - _____
- ✓ _____ - _____
- ✓ _____ - _____
- ✓ _____ - _____
- ✓ _____ - _____
- ✓ _____ - _____
- ✓ _____ - _____
- ✓ _____ - _____
- ✓ _____ - _____
- ✓ _____ - _____
- ✓ _____ - _____

Biblical Investigation about Your New Spiritual Hunger

I Peter 2:1-3

1. What does God want you to remove from your new spiritual life?
   1 Wherefore laying aside all <u>malice</u>, and all <u>guile</u>, and <u>hypocrisies</u>, and <u>envies</u>, and all evil <u>speakings</u>,

2. What does God want you to hunger for so that you can grow in your new spiritual life?
   <u>The sincere milk of the Word</u>

3. Why should you enjoy the Word of God?
   <u>For my growth</u>

4. Why should you have an appetite for God's Word?
   <u>Because I have tasted God's graciousness</u>

Romans 6:4

5. In what type of life does God want you to walk after you have accepted Jesus Christ as your Savior?
   <u>A new life</u>

Hebrews 5:12-14

6. The milk of God's Word is for what type of Christian?
   <u>Unskilled, baby</u>

7. What must you do so that you can enjoy the meat of God's Word?
   <u>Exercise (use) it</u>

Walk in Newness of Life

8. What will be the result of your being able to use the meat of God's Word?
   Discernment of good and evil

II Timothy 3:14-17

9. What has made you wise unto salvation?
   The Holy Scriptures

10. Who inspired the Scriptures?
    God

11. What are the Scriptures (the Bible) profitable for in your life?
    - For <u>doctrine</u>
    - For <u>reproof</u>
    - For <u>correction</u>
    - For <u>instruction</u> in righteousness

12. What are the results of allowing God's Word to work in your life?
    - You may be <u>perfect</u> (mature)
    - You may be throughly <u>furnished</u> unto all good works

Psalm 1:1-3

13. What three things must you not do so that you can be blessed by God?
    - <u>Walk</u> not in the counsel of the ungodly
    - <u>Stand</u> in the way of sinners
    - <u>Sit</u> in the seat of the scorner

14. What must be your delight, and on what must you meditate (think about) day and night so that you can be blessed by God?
    God's law (the Bible)

15. What will be the result of your rejecting sinfulness while thinking about and applying God's Word to your life?
    I will prosper

James 1:21-25

16. What two things must you lay aside?
    - Filthiness
    - Superfluity of naughtiness

17. What must you receive with meekness?
    The Word of God

18. After you hear God's Word, what must you do with it?
    Do it (obey it, apply it)

19. Will God bless you if you hear His Word but do not obey it?
    No

Psalm 119:72, 140

20. What should you consider God's Word to be better than?
    - Thousands of gold
    - Thousands of silver

21. Why should you love God's Word?
    Because it is pure

Psalm 19:7-11

22. Describe God's Word.
    7 The law of the LORD is <u>perfect</u>, converting the soul: the testimony of the LORD is <u>sure</u>, making wise the simple.
    8 The statutes of the LORD are <u>right</u>, rejoicing the heart: the commandment of the LORD is <u>pure</u>, enlightening the eyes.
    9 The fear of the LORD is <u>clean</u>, <u>enduring</u> for ever: the judgments of the LORD are <u>true</u> and <u>righteous</u> altogether.
    10 More to be <u>desired</u> are they than gold, yea, than much fine gold: <u>sweeter</u> also than honey and the honeycomb.
    11 Moreover by them is thy servant warned: and in keeping of them there is great reward.

23. Describe the results of God's Word in your life.
    7 The law of the LORD is perfect, <u>converting</u> the soul: the testimony of the LORD is sure, making <u>wise</u> the simple.
    8 The statutes of the LORD are right, <u>rejoicing</u> the heart: the commandment of the LORD is pure, <u>enlightening</u> the eyes.
    9 The fear of the LORD is clean, enduring for ever: the judgments of the LORD are true and righteous altogether.
    10 More to be desired are they than gold, yea, than much fine gold: sweeter also than honey and the honeycomb.
    11 Moreover by them is thy servant <u>warned</u>: and in keeping of them there is great <u>reward</u>.

Psalm 63:1-11

24. When should you seek for God?
    Early

25. When should you remember and meditate on God and His works?
    In my bed at night

Acts 17:10-11

26. How did the believers in Berea receive the Word of God?
    With readiness of mind

27. What did the believers do with the Word of God daily?
    Search the Scriptures

II Timothy 2:15

28. What must you do with the Word of God?
    *15 **Study** to shew thyself approved unto God, a workman that needeth not to be ashamed, rightly **dividing** the word of truth.*

Personal Notes about Your New Spiritual Hunger

Walk in Newness of Life

Chapter 10

Your New Access to the Throne of Grace

Hebrews 4:14-16
Seeing then that we have a great high priest,
that is passed into the heavens,
Jesus the Son of God, let us hold fast our profession.
For we have not an high priest which cannot be touched
with the feeling of our infirmities;
but was in all points tempted like as we are,
yet without sin.
Let us therefore come boldly unto the throne of grace,
that we may obtain mercy,
and find grace to help in time of need.

Chapter 10

Your New Access to the Throne of Grace

A Biblical Introduction to Your New Access to the Throne of Grace

Hebrews 4:14-16 encourages each believer in their time of need to "*come boldly unto the throne of grace, that [they] may obtain mercy, and find grace to help in time of need.*" Because we have a "*great high priest, that is passed into the heavens, Jesus the Son of God*" who can "*be touched with the feeling of our infirmities;*" because He "*was in all points tempted like as we are, yet without sin.*" Jesus Christ lived on this earth and experienced the same struggles and temptations that each person faces, but He never sinned. For this reason, He understands and desires to care for each of your needs and prayer requests in order to help you live holy during each of your life's situations. He encourages you to present your needs and prayer requests before the throne of grace so you can enjoy God's unlimited grace and mercy for each of your life's situations.

Jesus Christ wants you to be "*bold,*" or confident in asking Him for help. There is no cause for fear or timidity when you pray to God for help for any needs. The Apostle Paul taught believers to "*Be careful for nothing; but in every thing by prayer and supplication with thanksgiving let your requests be made known unto God. And the peace of God, which passeth all understanding, shall keep your hearts and minds through Christ Jesus*" (Philippians 4:6-7). There is nothing too big or too small to bring to the throne of grace in prayer, for God is the "*Father of mercies, and the God of all comfort; who comforteth us in all our tribulation, that we may be able to comfort them which are in any trouble, by the comfort wherewith we ourselves are comforted of God"* (II Corinthians 1:3-4).

James 1:5-7 clarifies the reason you must make your requests boldly before God by saying, "*If any of you lack wisdom, let him ask of God, that giveth to all men liberally, and upbraideth not; and it shall be given him. But let him ask in faith, nothing wavering. For he that wavereth is like a wave of the sea driven with the wind and tossed. For let not that man think that he shall receive any thing of the Lord.*" Your boldness in prayer is based on your faith that Jesus Christ has provided an entrance into God the Father's Holy of Holies. Hebrews 10:19-23 explains by saying, "*Having therefore, brethren, boldness to enter into the holiest by the blood of Jesus, by a new and living way, which he hath consecrated for us, through the veil, that is to say, his flesh; and having an high priest over the house of God; let us draw near with a true heart in full assurance of faith, having our hearts sprinkled from an evil conscience, and our bodies washed with pure water. Let us hold fast the profession of our faith without wavering; (for he is faithful that promised.)*" (Mark 15:37-38).

In His personal care for you and His desire for you to personally seek help at any time, for any reason, God has made His personal assistance available for you during your prayer time through the Holy Spirit. Romans 8:26 says, "*Likewise the Spirit also helpeth our infirmities: for we know not what we should pray for as we ought: but the Spirit itself maketh intercession for us with groanings which cannot be uttered.*" Even when you don't know what to pray for, or how to express the desires and burdens of your heart, God promises that the Holy Spirit will speak on your behalf and that God the Father will receive your requests.

In Luke 11:1, one of Jesus Christ's disciples, after observing Him pray on many occasions, said to Him "*Lord, teach us to pray, as John also taught his disciples.*" In verses 2-4, Jesus kindly responds by sharing with them "The Lord's Prayer," in which He provides four important subjects that should be included in your prayer time. First, He gave glory to God by saying, "*Our Father*

Your New Access to the Throne of Grace

which art in heaven, Hallowed be thy name." Second, He asked for God's will to be fulfilled by saying, "*Thy kingdom come. Thy will be done, as in heaven, so in earth.*" Third, He asked for personal physical needs by saying, "*Give us day by day our daily bread.*" Fourth, He asked for spiritual needs and protection by saying, "*And forgive us our sins; for we also forgive every one that is indebted to us. And lead us not into temptation; but deliver us from evil.*" Each of these four principles should be part of your prayers to God, as He deserves all the glory. He can be depended upon for all things.

After giving His disciples an example of prayer, Jesus continued to share God's faithfulness to answer prayer through two parables about asking and receiving (Luke 11:5-8, 11-13). He also reassured His disciples by saying, "*Ask, and it shall be given you; seek, and ye shall find; knock, and it shall be opened unto you. For every one that asketh receiveth; and he that seeketh findeth; and to him that knocketh it shall be opened*" (Luke 11:9-10). You must come before the throne of grace with confidence that God will always answer your request based on what He knows is best for you.

The Apostle Paul, after speaking about spiritual warfare and the armor of God for the believer in Ephesians 6:10-17, said in verses 18-20 that believers should be "*Praying always with all prayer and supplication in the Spirit, and watching thereunto with all perseverance and supplication for all saints; and for me, that utterance may be given unto me, that I may open my mouth boldly, to make known the mystery of the gospel, for which I am an ambassador in bonds: that therein I may speak boldly, as I ought to speak.*" He was very clear that believers should be praying for one another and for their spiritual leadership. In I Timothy 2:1-4, he also said, "*I exhort therefore, that, first of all, supplications, prayers, intercessions, and giving of thanks, be made for all men; for kings, and for all that are in authority; that we may lead a quiet and peaceable life in all godliness and honesty. For this is good and acceptable in the sight of God our Saviour; who will have all men to be saved, and to come unto the knowledge of the truth.*" Prayer should be made for political leaders and unbelievers in general, both for social tranquility and for their salvation through Jesus Christ.

In Matthew 6:5-8, before Jesus presented "The Lord's Prayer" to His disciples, He explained some important principles for prayer. In verses 5-6, He taught them not to pray in public for man's approval, but rather in private to receive God's blessing. In verses 7-8, He taught them to not pray with vain repetition because that is what unbelievers do, and He reassures them by saying, "*thy Father which is in secret; and thy Father which seeth in secret shall reward thee openly ... for your Father knoweth what things ye have need of, before ye ask him*" (Matthew 6:6, 8). You must trust God with each of your needs. You must believe that the God who saved your soul for all eternity can and will protect you and provide for each of life's situations on this earth. You must go boldly before "*the throne of grace, that [you] may obtain mercy, and find grace to help in time of need*" (Hebrews 4:16). You must "*Pray without ceasing. In every thing give thanks: for this is the will of God in Christ Jesus concerning you*" (I Thessalonians 5:17-18).

Biblical Instruction about
Your New Access to the Throne of Grace

- ✓ **Matthew 18:19-20, Acts 1:13-14** - Believers should enjoy the opportunity to pray together.

- ✓ **Luke 18:1-8** - Believers should be fervent and faithful in prayer.

- ✓ **John 15:7, I John 3:22** - Believers should be assured that when they follow God's Word, God will answer their prayers.

- ✓ **Ephesians 6:18-20** - Believers should pray for each other and for spiritual leadership.

- ✓ **Colossians 4:2** - Believers should continue in prayer with thanksgiving.

- ✓ **James 4:1-3** - Believers lack what they desire or need when they neglect to pray or misuse prayer.

- ✓ **James 5:14-18** - Believers should request prayer for those who are sick.

- ✓ **I John 5:14-15** - Believers should be assured that when they pray according to God's will, He will hear their requests.

- ✓ **I Timothy 2:1-4, 8** - Believers should pray for all men, including governmental leaders.

- ✓ _____ - _____
  _____

77

Walk in Newness of Life

- ✓ _____ - _____
- ✓ _____ - _____
- ✓ _____ - _____
- ✓ _____ - _____
- ✓ _____ - _____
- ✓ _____ - _____
- ✓ _____ - _____
- ✓ _____ - _____
- ✓ _____ - _____
- ✓ _____ - _____
- ✓ _____ - _____
- ✓ _____ - _____

Biblical Investigation about Your New Access to the Throne of Grace

Hebrews 4:14-16

1. Who is your Great High Priest?
   Jesus Christ

2. Does your Great High Priest know and understand your daily struggles?
   Yes

3. How should you come before the Throne of Grace with your prayer requests and needs?
   Boldly

4. What does Jesus Christ provide you when you present yourself before the Throne of Grace?
   - Mercy
   - Grace

Philippians 4:6-7

5. For what should you pray?
   Everything

6. What does God offer you when you share your requests with Him?
   Peace that passes all understanding

II Corinthians 1:3-4

7. Who is the Father of mercies and the God of all comfort?
   God the Father

8. For what tribulations does God offer you His comfort?
   All

James 1:5-7

9. What are you commanded to do if you lack wisdom?
   Ask God

10. How does God provide you wisdom when you ask Him for it?
    Liberally

11. How must you ask God for wisdom?
    In faith, nothing wavering

Hebrews 10:19-23

12. How may you enter the Holy of Holies for your prayer time?
    Boldly

13. What price was paid to make the Holy of Holies open for you to enter into?
    Jesus Christ's blood

14. Is God faithful to keep His promises to save and care for you?
    Yes

Your New Access to the Throne of Grace

Romans 8:26

15. Who helps you when you do not know how to pray?
    The Holy Spirit

Luke 11:1-13

16. What was the example of prayer that Jesus gave to His disciples to teach them to pray?
    2 And he said unto them, When ye pray, say, Our <u>Father</u> which art in heaven, <u>Hallowed</u> be thy name. Thy <u>kingdom</u> come. Thy <u>will</u> be done, as in heaven, so in earth.
    3 Give us day by day our daily <u>bread</u>.
    4 And <u>forgive</u> us our sins; for we also forgive every one that is indebted to us. And <u>lead</u> us not into temptation; but <u>deliver</u> us from evil.

17. What two parable did Jesus give to His disciples to teach them about God's willingness to hear and answer their requests?
    ♦ The parable of a friend
    ♦ The Parable of a son and father

18. Will God provide for your needs if you will ask Him for His help?
    Yes

Matthew 6:5-8

19. Should you pray to be seen of men or heard by God?
    Heard by God

20. Should you use vain repetition in your prayers?
    No

21. Does God know your needs?
    Yes

I Thessalonians 5:17-18

22. Should you ever cease praying to God?
    No

23. For what things should you thank God?
    Everything

Personal Notes about
Your New Access to the Throne of Grace

Walk in Newness of Life

Chapter 11

Your Body's New Owner

I Corinthians 6:19-20
What? know ye not that your body
is the temple of the Holy Ghost
which is in you, which ye have of God,
and ye are not your own?
For ye are bought with a price:
therefore glorify God in your body,
and in your spirit, which are God's.

Chapter 11

Your Body's New Owner

A Biblical Introduction to Your Body's New Owner

I Corinthians 6:19-20 is quite clear that after you receive Jesus Christ as your personal Savior and begin your new life, your body does not belong to you any longer. It says, "*Ye are not your own*" because "*ye are bought with a price.*" The price paid for your life, body, and soul was not of this world's goods, but rather "*the precious blood of Christ, as of a lamb without blemish and without spot*" (I Peter 1:18-19). With that payment, God has purchased the rights to live in and work through your body. He has declared that "*your body is the temple of the Holy Ghost*" (I Corinthians 6:19). At the very moment of your faith in Jesus Christ, God sent you a Comforter, the Holy Spirit (John 14:15-17, *as was studied in chapter 3, Your New Comforter*). This Comforter lives in you, and wants to help you glorify God with every part of your being while you are still living on earth. Because God has lovingly chosen to live in you and make your body His temple, you should gladly "*glorify God in your body, and in your spirit, which are God's*" (I Corinthians 6:20).

At the moment of your salvation, you became "*a new creature: old things [were] passed away; behold, all things [were] become new*" (II Corinthians 5:17). With overwhelming appreciation for the new life God has given you, you should say with the Apostle Paul, "*According to my earnest expectation and my hope, that in nothing I shall be ashamed, but that with all boldness, as always, so now also Christ shall be magnified in my body, whether it be by life, or by death. For to me to live is Christ, and to die is gain*" (Philippians 1:20-21). Glorifying God with your every thought, word, and action should be your greatest goal. It

Walk in Newness of Life

should be what motivates you to do what is holy and prevents you from doing what is sinful. Romans 6:12-13 says it this way, "*Let not sin therefore reign in your mortal body, that ye should obey it in the lusts thereof. Neither yield ye your members as instruments of unrighteousness unto sin: but yield yourselves unto God, as those that are alive from the dead, and your members as instruments of righteousness unto God.*"

In Romans 12:1-2, the Apostle Paul pleads with fellow believers to "*present [their] bodies a living sacrifice, holy, acceptable unto God, which is your reasonable service. And be not conformed to this world: but be ye transformed by the renewing of [their] mind, that ye may prove what is that good, and acceptable, and perfect, will of God.*" Just as a sacrifice is offered in reverence and worship of God, you must live your life in reverence and worship of God by only allowing your body to be used for His glory. You must allow the Holy Spirit to have authority over your body and to guide you through God's Word so that you do not defile His temple (I Corinthians 3:16-17). You should not allow God's temple to be contaminated with worldly things, thoughts, or actions (II Corinthians 6:15-18). For you to keep God's temple pure, you must learn self-control and spiritual discipline. You must say with the Apostle Paul, "*I keep under my body, and bring it into subjection: lest that by any means, when I have preached to others, I myself should be a castaway*" (I Corinthians 9:27). You must seek to always be "*accepted of him. For we must all appear before the judgment seat of Christ; that every one may receive the things done in his body, according to that he hath done, whether it be good or bad*" (II Corinthians 5:9-10, Ecclesiastes 12:13-14). You must dedicate yourself so that "*Whether therefore ye eat, or drink, or whatsoever ye do, [ye] do all to the glory of God*" (I Corinthians 10:31).

Biblical Instruction about Your Body's New Owner

✓ **Romans 6:11-22** - Each believer must choose to serve God with their body rather than serve sin.

✓ **II Corinthians 4:10-11** - Each believer must choose to allow Jesus Christ to live through their body.

✓ **Philippians 1:20** - Each believer must choose to use their body to glorify Jesus Christ in life or death.

✓ **I Thessalonians 5:23** - Each believer must strive to keep their body pure until Jesus Christ's coming.

✓ **I Peter 4:1-2** - Each believer must choose to use their body to fulfill God's will instead of man's lusts.

✓ _____ - _____

✓ _____ - _____

✓ _____ - _____

✓ _____ - _____

✓ _____ - _____

Walk in Newness of Life

- ✓ _____ - _____
- ✓ _____ - _____
- ✓ _____ - _____
- ✓ _____ - _____
- ✓ _____ - _____
- ✓ _____ - _____
- ✓ _____ - _____
- ✓ _____ - _____
- ✓ _____ - _____
- ✓ _____ - _____
- ✓ _____ - _____

Biblical Investigation about Your Body's New Owner

I Corinthians 6:19-20

1. Your body is Who's temple after your salvation?
   The Holy Spirit's

2. Who is the owner of your body?
   God

3. With what should you glorify God?
   ♦ Your body
   ♦ Your spirit

I Peter 1:18-19

4. What price was paid for your life?
   Jesus Christ's blood

John 14:15-17

5. What does your obedience to God prove?
   My love for Him

6. Who has God given you to abide in your body after salvation?
   The Holy Spirit

Walk in Newness of Life

II Corinthians 5:17

7. What has God made you at your salvation?
   A new creature

Philippians 1:20-21

8. Who should be magnified (glorified) with your body?
   Jesus Christ

Romans 6:12-13

9. What should not have authority over your body?
   Sin

10. What should you not do with your body?
    Unrighteousness

11. What should you yield your body to do?
    Righteousness

Romans 12:1-2

12. How should you present your body to God?
    As a living sacrifice - holy

13. What type of service is your living for God?
    Reasonable

Your Body's New Owner

14. What are the two parts to doing the good, and acceptable, and perfect will of God for your life?
    - ◆ Be not conformed to this world
    - ◆ Be transformed by the renewing of my mind

I Corinthians 3:16-17

15. How should you maintain your body because it is the temple of the Holy Spirit?
    Holy

I Corinthians 9:27

16. Why should you keep your body under subjection?
    So that I am not a castaway (bad testimony)

I Corinthians 5:9-10

17. To Whom will you give an account for what you do with our body?
    Jesus Christ

I Corinthians 10:31

18. When should you glorify God with your body?
    - ◆ Eating
    - ◆ Drinking
    - ◆ Whatever I do

Personal Notes about Your Body's New Owner

Walk in Newness of Life

Chapter 12

Your New Lifestyle

Ephesians 4:20-24
But ye have not so learned Christ;
if so be that ye have heard him,
and have been taught by him, as the truth is in Jesus:
That ye put off concerning the former conversation
the old man,
which is corrupt according to the deceitful lusts;
And be renewed in the spirit of your mind;
And that ye put on the new man,
which after God is created in righteousness
and true holiness.

Chapter 12

Your New Lifestyle

A Biblical Introduction to Your New Lifestyle

In Ephesians 4:17-24, the Apostle Paul authoritatively teaches that you must separate yourself from your old lifestyle and begin applying a new one that follows after God's holiness. He says, "***This I say therefore, and testify in the Lord, that ye henceforth walk not as other Gentiles walk, in the vanity of their mind, ... But ye have not so learned Christ; ... put off concerning the former conversation the old man, ... put on the new man, which after God is created in righteousness and true holiness.***" This process of transformation must begin with a renovation of your way of thinking (as studied in chapter 8, *Your New Mind*), which will naturally result in a transformation of your speech, attitudes, and actions (Ephesians 4:17-23, Romans 12:1-3). As you are "*taught by*" Jesus Christ and the salvation He has provided you, will learn that you must always be "**denying ungodliness and worldly lusts,** [and that you] ***should live soberly, righteously, and godly, in this present world; looking for that blessed hope, and the glorious appearing of the great God and our Saviour Jesus Christ; Who gave himself for us, that he might redeem us from all iniquity, and purify unto himself a peculiar people, zealous of good works***" (Titus 2:11-14, 3:1, 8, 14).

You were born with an "*old man,*" or sin nature, which was "*corrupt according to the deceitful lusts*" (Ephesians 4:22); but when you accepted Jesus Christ as your personal Savior, your "***old man [was] crucified with him, that the body of sin might be destroyed, that henceforth [you] should not serve sin***" (Romans 6:6). At the very moment you believed in Jesus Christ, you became "***a new creature: old things [were] passed away; behold, all things***

87

Walk in Newness of Life

[were] ***become new***" (II Corinthians 5:17). You were also given a "***new man, which after God is created in righteousness and true holiness***" (Ephesians 4:24). Therefore, you must choose to live according to your new man by rejecting the old man and his sinful lifestyle or habits. As you remove the old man's habits of living for self and begin to replace them with Jesus Christ's teachings and example, you will begin to enjoy a new life of holiness. I Peter 2:21-24 says, "***Christ also suffered for us, leaving us an example, that ye should follow his steps: Who did no sin, neither was guile found in his mouth: Who, when he was reviled, reviled not again; when he suffered, he threatened not; but committed himself to him that judgeth righteously: Who his own self bare our sins in his own body on the tree, that we, being dead to sins, should live unto righteousness: by whose stripes ye were healed.***"

The Apostle Paul's instruction about removing the old man while applying the new man can be divided into three different parts: your speech, your attitudes, and your actions. If you are to truly change your old, sinful lifestyle for your new, holy lifestyle, you must dedicate yourself to remove any speech, attitudes, and actions that do not please God and replace them with speech, attitudes, and actions that do please God.

First, you must choose your style of speech. The Apostle Paul is very clear, you must put "***away lying***" and replace it with "***truth***" (Ephesians 4:25). You must "***let no corrupt communication proceed out of your mouth,***" but rather speak "***that which is good to the use of edifying, that it may minister grace unto the hearers***" (Ephesians 4:29). You must eliminate any "***clamour [or shouting] and evil speaking [or damaging words],***" and replace it with kindness and forgiveness (Ephesians 4:31-32). You must guard your tongue so that "***filthiness [or shameful], nor foolish talking, nor jesting, which are not convenient***" are not part of your style of communication, but rather a continual "***giving of thanks***" (Ephesians 5:4). You must recognize that "***it is a shame even to speak of those ... unfruitful works of darkness ... which are done of them in secret***" (Ephesians 5:11-12).

Your New Lifestyle

The words of your mouth reveal your heart. Jesus Christ said, *"A good man out of the good treasure of his heart bringeth forth that which is good; and an evil man out of the evil treasure of his heart bringeth forth that which is evil: for of the abundance of the heart his mouth speaketh"* (Luke 6:45). Your tongue is powerful, and can be used for great good or terrible destruction (James 3:2-12). You must work hard to remove your old way of speaking so that you can *"let your speech be alway with grace, seasoned with salt, that ye may know how ye ought to answer every man"* (Colossians 4:6).

Second, you must choose your style of attitude by conscientiously doing away with selfishness as you seek the best interest of others. You must begin by being sure that when you are *"angry,"* you *"sin not"* (Ephesians 4:26). You must dedicate yourself to not let *"the sun go down upon your wrath"* by holding on to your frustration and irritation with others, understanding that when you do, you are giving *"place to the devil"* (Ephesians 4:26-27). Then you must *"Let all bitterness, and wrath, and anger, ... be put away from you,"* *"or covetousness"* by purposely being *"kind one to another, tenderhearted, forgiving one another, even as God for Christ's sake hath forgiven you"* (Ephesians 4:31-32, 5:3).

Your attitude toward circumstances and people reveals your level of humility and pride. You must accept that God allows each circumstance and person into your life for your benefit, and therefore you must trust Him with each one (Romans 8:28). You must choose to *"be subject one to another, and be clothed with humility: for God resisteth the proud, and giveth grace to the humble. Humble yourselves therefore under the mighty hand of God, that he may exalt you in due time: Casting all your care upon him; for he careth for you"* (I Peter 5:5-7).

Third, you must choose your style of actions by having self-control over all of your body. You must be careful to not *"steal"* others possessions, time, etc. *"but rather ... labor, working with [your] hands the thing which is good, that [you] may have to give to him that needeth"* (Ephesians 4:28). You must remove any type of *"malice"* or maliciousness towards others by being *"kind one to another"* (Ephesians 4:31-32). You must also separate yourself from

Walk in Newness of Life

all "*fornication, and all uncleanness,*" and "*let it not be once named among you, as becometh saints*" (Ephesians 5:3). "*Be not ye therefore partakers with them. For ye were sometimes darkness, but now are ye light in the Lord: walk as children of light: (For the fruit of the Spirit is in all goodness and righteousness and truth;) proving what is acceptable unto the Lord. And have no fellowship with the unfruitful works of darkness, but rather reprove them*" (Ephesians 5:7-11).

Your new actions will reveal to those around you that you are one of God's children . You must "*Let your light so shine before men, that they may see your good works, and glorify your Father which is in heaven*" (Matthew 5:16). You must say with the Apostle Paul, "*But I keep under my body, and bring it into subjection: lest that by any means, when I have preached to others, I myself should be a castaway*" (I Corinthians 9:27).

At the time of your salvation, God not only saved your soul and gave you a home in heaven, He also provided for you to have an entirely new lifestyle: a lifestyle that follows "*after righteousness, godliness, faith love, patience, meekness,*" and receives His blessing (I Timothy 6:11). He desires that you "*might have life,*" and that you "*might have it mor abundantly*" (John 10:10). Therefore, you must "*put ye on the Lord Jesus Christ, and make not provision for the flesh, to fulfil the lusts thereof*" (Romans 13:14). You must carefully and purposefully live each moment, with each word, each attitude, and each action for the glory of God.

Biblical Instruction about Your New Lifestyle

✓ **Matthew 12:43-45** - Each believer must diligently replace his old sinful lifestyle with a new godly lifestyle.

✓ **Romans 8:1-13** - Each believer must choose to follow the leading of the Holy Spirit and depend on His power to help them eliminate their old lifestyle.

✓ **Romans 13:11-14** - Each believer must seek to follow Jesus Christ in their new lifestyle by carefully preventing opportunities to fulfill the lusts of the flesh.

✓ **Galatians 6:7-9** - Each believer will receive fruit (reward or punishment) for their lifestyle.

✓ **Colossians 1:9-14, 2:6-8, 3:5-17** - Each believer must choose to put off his old lifestyle of sin and put on his new lifestyle of righteousness based on his new life in Jesus Christ.

✓ **I Thessalonians 4:1-8** - Each believer must chose to live a pure lifestyle so as to please God the Father.

✓ _____ - _____

✓ _____ - _____

✓ _____ - _____

Walk in Newness of Life

- ✓ _____ - _____
- ✓ _____ - _____
- ✓ _____ - _____
- ✓ _____ - _____
- ✓ _____ - _____
- ✓ _____ - _____
- ✓ _____ - _____
- ✓ _____ - _____
- ✓ _____ - _____
- ✓ _____ - _____
- ✓ _____ - _____

Biblical Investigation about Your New Lifestyle

Ephesians 4:17-24

1. How should you not walk in your new lifestyle?
   In the vanity of my mind

2. What has Jesus Christ taught you to put off?
   The old man and his ways

3. What has Jesus Christ taught you to put on?
   The new man in righteousness and holiness

Romans 12:1-3

4. What type of living sacrifice should your new lifestyle represent?
   - Holy
   - Acceptable

Titus 2:11-14, 3:1, 8, 14

5. How has the grace of salvation taught you to live?
   11 For the grace of God that bringeth salvation hath appeared to all men,
   12 Teaching us that, denying <u>ungodliness</u> and worldly <u>lusts</u>, we should live <u>soberly</u>, <u>righteously</u>, and <u>godly</u>, in this present world;
   13 <u>Looking</u> for that blessed hope, and the glorious appearing of the great God and our Saviour Jesus Christ;

Romans 6:6

6. Who was crucified with Christ?
   The old man

7. Should you continue to serve sin?
   No

II Corinthians 5:17

8. What things have passed away when you accepted Jesus Christ as your Savior?
   All things

I Peter 2:21-24

9. Whose example should you follow in your new lifestyle?
   Jesus Christ's

Ephesians 4:25, 29, 31-32

10. What should you speak in your new lifestyle?
    The truth

11. What type of speech should you have in your new lifestyle?
    That which edifies others

12. What types of speaking should you put away from you in your new lifestyle?
    ♦ Clamour
    ♦ Evil speaking

Your New Lifestyle

Ephesians 5:4, 11-12

13. What types of speech should not be part of your new lifestyle?
    - ◆ Filthiness
    - ◆ Foolish talking
    - ◆ Jesting

14. What type of speech should you include in your new lifestyle?
    Giving of thanks

15. Should you speak of sinful things done in secret?
    No

Luke 6:45

16. What does your speech reveal about you?
    My heart

James 3:2-12

17. Is it easy to offend others with your speech?
    Yes

18. Must you work hard to control your speech?
    Yes

Colossians 4:6

19. What types of speech should you have?
    6 Let your speech be alway with <u>grace</u>, seasoned with <u>salt</u>, that ye may know how ye ought to answer every man.

Ephesians 4:26-27, 31-32, 5:3

20. Should you remain angry in your new lifestyle?
    No

21. Who has an opportunity to destroy your life if you live in anger?
    The Devil

22. What attitudes should you eliminate from your new lifestyle?
    - Bitterness
    - Wrath
    - Anger
    - Covetousness

23. What attitudes should you include in your new lifestyle?
    - Kindness
    - Tenderheartedness
    - Forgiveness

I Peter 5:5-7

24. Who will God lift up in due time?
    The humble

25. Who does God resist?
    The proud

Ephesians 4:28, 31-32

26. What should you never do in your new lifestyle?
    Steal

Your New Lifestyle

27. What should you do with your hands in your new lifestyle?
    Work to do good for others

28. Should you do any malice (malicious deeds) to others in your new lifestyle?
    No

Ephesians 5:3, 7-11

29. What types of sins should never be part of your new lifestyle?
    - Fornication
    - All uncleanness
    - All covetousness

30. How should you walk in your new lifestyle?
    As a child of light

31. Should you have any fellowship with the unfruitful works of darkness?
    No - Should reprove them

Matthew 5:16

32. Who should receive the glory from your new lifestyle of good works?
    God the Father

I Corinthians 9:27

33. How must you keep your body so that you are not a spiritual castaway?
    Under subjection

John 10:10

34. What type of life does God want you to have?
    And abundant life

Romans 13:14

35. Whose life should your new lifestyle represent?
    Jesus Christ's

36. Should you give any opportunity for your flesh to fulfill its lusts in your new lifestyle?
    No

Personal Notes about Your New Lifestyle

Chapter 13

Your New Privilege

II Corinthians 5:17-18
Therefore if any man be in Christ,
he is a new creature: old things are passed away;
behold, all things are become new.
And all things are of God,
who hath reconciled us to himself by Jesus Christ,
and hath given to us the ministry of reconciliation;
To wit, that God was in Christ,
reconciling the world unto himself,
not imputing their trespasses unto them;
and hath committed unto us the word of reconciliation.
Now then we are ambassadors for Christ,
as though God did beseech you by us:
we pray you in Christ's stead, be ye reconciled to God.
For he hath made him to be sin for us,
who knew no sin;
that we might be made the righteousness of God in him.

Chapter 13

Your New Privilege

A Biblical Introduction to Your New Privilege

II Corinthians 5:17 reveals a wonderful truth about the spiritual change God made in your life at the very moment you accepted Jesus Christ as your personal Savior when it says, "***Therefore if any man be in Christ, he is a new creature: old things are passed away; behold, all things are become new.***" God has given you a new life, with new privileges. However, with each privilege there is great responsibility. One of the greatest privileges you have been given is found in II Corinthians 5:20, where the Apostle Paul firmly declares, "***Now then we are ambassadors for Christ ...***"

God's plan for your life was not limited to forgiving your sins and giving you a home in heaven. He desires to make your life on this earth of eternal value by allowing you to participate in sharing His message of reconciliation (peace) with your family, friends, acquaintances, and even strangers, so that they can also enjoy a new life of reconciliation with Him.

The Apostle Paul explains the privilege of being God's ambassador in II Corinthians 5:18-20. He starts by establishing God's authority over your life. Verse 18 begins by saying, "***And all things are of God, who hath reconciled us to himself by Jesus Christ.***" God has given you a physical life by permitting you to be born into this physical world, and therefore has authority over your physical life. He has also given you spiritual life through your spiritual birth, and therefore has authority over your spiritual life (Juan 3:1-8). God's love for you, displayed in Jesus Christ's sacrifice on the cross to reconcile your sin debt and provide you peace with Him, should motivate you to faithfully serve Him until

Walk in Newness of Life

He chooses to take you home to be with Him in heaven. Therefore, you should say with the Apostle Paul, *"For the love of Christ constraineth us; because we thus judge, that if one died for all, then were all dead: And that he died for all, that they which live should not henceforth live unto themselves, but unto him which died for them, and rose again"* (II Corinthians 5:14-15). *"Forasmuch as ye know that ye were not redeemed with corruptible things, as silver and gold, from your vain conversation received by tradition from your fathers; but with the precious blood of Christ, as of a lamb without blemish and without spot"* (I Peter 1:18-19). *"For ye are bought with a price: therefore glorify God in your body, and in your spirit, which are God's"* (I Corinthians 6:20).

The Apostle Paul, after establishing God's authority and your peace with Him, continues in verse 18 by saying, *"and hath given to us the ministry of reconciliation."* At the very moment you accepted Jesus Christ as your personal Savior, you were reconciled to God and given a ministry. Your ministry is to serve God by serving His message of love and peace to those around you. God desires that the entire world would have the opportunity to be at peace with Him just as you are (II Peter 3:9). He even sent angels to earth on the evening of Christ's birth to proclaim *"Glory to God in the highest, and on earth peace, good will toward men"* (Luke 2:14). Jesus Christ, as he ascended into heaven after His death and resurrection, commanded His disciples by saying, *"Go ye therefore, and teach all nations, baptizing them in the name of the Father, and of the Son, and of the Holy Ghost: teaching them to observe all things whatsoever I have commanded you: and, lo, I am with you alway, even unto the end of the world. Amen"* (Matthew 28:19-20).

You have been given a ministry of reconciliation. Your ministry of reconciliation requires that you faithfully serve those around you by sharing God's solution to their sinful condition through faith in the finished work of Jesus Christ with them. *"For whosoever shall call upon the name of the Lord shall be saved. How then shall they call on him in whom they have not believed?*

Your New Privilege

and how shall they believe in him of whom they have not heard? and how shall they hear without a preacher? And how shall they preach, except they be sent? as it is written, How beautiful are the feet of them that preach the gospel of peace, and bring glad tidings of good things" (Romans 10:13-15)!

The Apostle Paul continues to speak of the ministry of reconciliation by saying in verse 19, "*To wit, that God was in Christ, reconciling the world unto himself, not imputing their trespasses unto them.*" God has entrusted you with His great message of reconciliation to share with the world. Will you say with the Apostle Paul, "*Therefore seeing we have this ministry, as we have received mercy, we faint not; but have renounced the hidden things of dishonesty, not walking in craftiness, nor handling the word of God deceitfully; but by manifestation of the truth commending ourselves to every man's conscience in the sight of God. But if our gospel be hid, it is hid to them that are lost: in whom the god of this world hath blinded the minds of them which believe not, lest the light of the glorious gospel of Christ, who is the image of God, should shine unto them. For we preach not ourselves, but Christ Jesus the Lord; and ourselves your servants for Jesus' sake*" (II Corinthians 4:1-5)?

Finally, at the end of verse 19, the Apostle Paul concludes by saying, "*and hath committed unto us the word of reconciliation.*" God has given you the manual for both how you should minister for Him and the message you must share with those around you. You have been given the Word of reconciliation through the Holy Scriptures, the Bible. The Bible is God's peace treaty to the world. Within its pages, God has revealed Who He is, how man has failed Him, and how man can have his relationship with Him restored through Jesus Christ (Romans 3:23, 5:8, 6:23, 10:9-10). Now you must dedicate yourself to read God's Word, learn God's Word, and share God's Word with those around you.

You have been given the greatest privilege mankind has ever enjoyed. You are the Creator's ambassador. You have His message to share with those you love and care for, but you must choose to remember His authority over your life. You must appreciate the price

Walk in Newness of Life

that he paid to reconcile you to Him. You must accept the ministry of reconciliation He has given you, and you must personally learn and share the Word of reconciliation so as to properly represent Him to the world around you.

Your New Privilege

Biblical Instruction about
Your New Purpose

- ✓ **Matthew 5:13-16** - Each believer is the spiritual salt and light of God to those around him so that they can taste and see God's loving salvation and desire a personal relationship with Him.

- ✓ **John 20:21** - Each believer has been sent into the world by Jesus Christ, just as He was sent by God the Father.

- ✓ **Acts 1:8** - Each believer has received the Holy Spirit to empower him to fulfill his ministry sharing the Gospel with the whole world.

- ✓ **I Corinthians 15:33-34** - Each believer must separate himself from any sinful influences that would prevent them from being able to share his knowledge of God with those around him.

- ✓ **II Corinthians 4:1-7** - Each believer has received a ministry which must be fulfilled by the mercy of God in purity so that the light of the Gospel can shine brightly before those around him.

- ✓ **I Peter 3:15** - Each believer must place God in first place in his life so that those around thim will ask about his faith, and he will have the opportunity to share the good news of the Gospel.

- ✓ _____ - _____
  _____

- ✓ _____ - _____
  _____

Walk in Newness of Life

- ✓ _____ - _____
- ✓ _____ - _____
- ✓ _____ - _____
- ✓ _____ - _____
- ✓ _____ - _____
- ✓ _____ - _____
- ✓ _____ - _____
- ✓ _____ - _____
- ✓ _____ - _____
- ✓ _____ - _____
- ✓ _____ - _____
- ✓ _____ - _____

Biblical Investigation about Your New Purpose

II Corinthians 5:17-20

1. What do you become when you accept Jesus Christ as your personal Savior?
   A new creature

2. How much of your life belongs to God after you are reconciled to Him through Jesus Christ?
   All of it

3. What ministry has God given you after you salvation?
   Reconciliation

4. What does God want to do for the world?
   Reconcile it to Himself

5. Who has God given the message of reconciliation to so that it can be shared with the world?
   Believers - new creatures in Christ

6. What is your new purpose (spiritual vocation) after your salvation?
   God's ambassador

II Corinthians 5:14-15

7. What should motivate you to fulfill God's purpose for your life?
   Christ's love

Walk in Newness of Life

8. For Whom should you live after your salvation?
   Jesus Christ

I Peter 1:18-19

9. What price was paid to redeem you from your sins?
   Jesus Christ's blood

I Corinthians 6:20

10. Why should you glorify God with your body and spirit?
    He paid for me and I am His

II Peter 3:9

11. Does God desire for anyone to perish?
    No

Luke 2:14

12. What does God want the earth to enjoy?
    Peace

Matthew 28:19-20

13. Where should you go to share the Gospel of Jesus Christ?
    To all nations

Your New Privilege

14. What should you teach those who will listen?
    <u>To be disciples of Jesus Christ and observe His commandments</u>

Romans 10:13-15

15. Who will God save?
    <u>Those who call on (believe in) Jesus Christ's name</u>

16. What is God's process for seeing the world saved?
    14 How then shall they <u>call</u> on him in whom they have not believed? and how shall they <u>believe</u> in him of whom they have not heard? and how shall they <u>hear</u> without a preacher?
    15 And how shall they <u>preach</u>, except they be <u>sent</u>? as it is written, How beautiful are the feet of them that preach the gospel of peace, and bring glad tidings of good things!

17. What does God consider the feet of those who share God's message of good news?
    <u>Beautiful</u>

II Corinthians 4:1-5

18. What has God given so that you do not faint (fail) in your purpose of ministry?
    <u>His mercy</u>

19. How must you go about fulfilling your ministry for God to those around you?
    2 But have renounced the hidden things of <u>dishonesty</u>, not walking in <u>craftiness</u>, nor handling the word of God <u>deceitfully</u>; but by manifestation of the <u>truth</u> commending ourselves to every man's <u>conscience</u> in the sight of <u>God</u>.

Walk in Newness of Life

20. Who loses the opportunity to receive the Gospel if you do not properly fulfill your ministry?
    The lost

21. Who seeks to blind the spiritual eyes of the lost so that they cannot see the light of the Gospel?
    The god of this world (Satan)

22. Who must you preach to the world around you?
    Christ Jesus the Lord

23. What are you to be to those with whom you share Jesus Christ?
    A servant for Jesus' sake

Romans 3:23, 5:6-10, 6:23, 10:9-10

24. Who has sinned and come short of God's glory (3:23)
    All people

25. What did God do to show His love for each sinner? (5:6-10)
    He sent His Son to die for them

26. What is the wage of sin? (6:23)
    Death

27. What has God offered to each sinner as a gift? (6:23)
    Eternal life

28. How can a sinner be saved from his sin? (10:9-10)
    9 That if thou shalt <u>confess</u> with thy mouth the Lord Jesus, and shalt <u>believe</u> in thine heart that God hath raised him from the dead, thou shalt be saved.
    10 For with the <u>heart</u> man believeth unto righteousness; and with the <u>mouth</u> confession is made unto salvation.

Personal Notes about Your New Privilege

Walk in Newness of Life

Other Ministry Resources Available from Walking in the WORD Ministries

Marriage: A Covenant Before God presents 10 biblical studies about marriage, each one is based on the marital relationship of Adam and Eve and has the purpose of helping young couples understand God's plan and purpose for their life together. Included are practical questions, illustrations, and applications for each biblical truth in order that the couple might grow in their knowledge of each other and how they can glorify God together.

Parenting with Purpose seeks to help young parents to spiritually prepare for the great privilege they have to care for and guide the life of one of God's precious creations. The first three lessons focus on the parents' need to honor God with their child, while the final three lessons focus on the parents' opportunity to represent God the Father to their child.

The Armor of God for Your Daily Battles provides a daily Bible study to review the spiritual resources God has provided for each believer so that they can enjoy a victorious Christian life.

The Calvary Road: Outline Guide was written to enhance your ability to understand, remember, and apply the important spiritual truths shared by Roy Hession in his book, The Calvary Road. After reading each chapter, you can review its content by filling in the blanks, considering the additional passages provided, and answering the reflection and application questions. Throughout this outline guide there are a few special features to help you focus on the truths being taught.

What Does the Bible Say About Salvation, Baptism, and Church Membership? provides a brief Biblical explanation for these three important subjects in the Christian life. Following each study are questions to help review each subject. These studies can be used with a new believer or pre-baptism or pre-church membership classes.

Missions: Ministering Beyond Our Borders was written to provide insight into the physical, emotional, and spiritual adjustments a missionary faces as he begins his new life and ministry. Throughout its pages you will find spiritual encouragements for the missionary and helpful hints for his family and friends who desire to support him in his service to their Lord and Savior Jesus Christ. There is also a "Missionary Edition," which provides a large appendix with additional tips specifically for missionaries.

The Deputation Trail: Ministry or a Means to an End? was written to help missionaries during their pre-field ministry by presenting biblically-based philosophies and practical tips to guide them through a God-honoring, church-expanding, and believer-edifying, deputation ministry.

The Heart of Man contains 12 Bible studies about the condition of man's heart and his need to allow God to provide salvation, help him take the first steps of Christian obedience, and give him security in his new relationship with God the Father as one of His children.

**Please visit
www.walkinginthewordministries.net
to find more biblical resources in English and Spanish.**

www.ingramcontent.com/pod-product-compliance
Lightning Source LLC
Chambersburg PA
CBHW081456040426
42446CB00016B/3261